Mathematics Olympiad

Class 02

A must have book for all
Olympiads & Talent Search Exams...

by
Niharika

BLoOM CAP
Bloom Cap Edu Ventures Pvt. Ltd.

Bloom Cap Edu Ventures Pvt. Ltd.

卐 **Administrative & Production Office**

'Ramchhaya' 4577/15, Agarwal Road, Darya Ganj, New Delhi -110002
Tele: 011- 47630600, 43518550

卐 ISBN : 978-93-25519-11-4

卐 PRICE : ₹100.00

卐 PO No : TXT-XX-XXXXXXX-X-XX

For further information about the books log on to
www.bloomcap.org

Follow us on 

Preface

"Future belongs to those Who prepares for it today"

School Olympiads are National & International level competitions conducted by different Government, Non-Government & Educational Organisations with the purpose of making the children ready to face competitive exams. The challenging Questions asked in Olympiads motivate them to learn more & more and bring out the best result with improved academic performance. The Awards & Scholarship offered in Olympiads motivate children to aspire & strive for doing better and emerge out to be the best.

Maths Olympiads

Mathematics is an integral part of all competitive exams be it Aptitude or Commerce or Science. Maths Olympiads are meant to develop Mathematical aptitude in school students. They provide students with an opportunity to master their concepts and comprehend tricky questions effortlessly. Challenging Questions of Maths Olympiads encourage students to develop a logical approach to solve Mathematical Problems.

'Bloom Mathematics Olympiad Study Book Class 2' is a perfect resource to Study & Practice for Olympiad Exams and other National & State Level Talent Search Exams & Other Competitions.

Some Special Features of Bloom Maths Olympiad Study Books are;

- Chapterwise Exercises having different types of Objective Questions at par with the Olympiad Level.
- Detailed Explanation for each question.
- Olympiad Pattern Practice Sets at the end.

This book is prepared by Expert Panel with the utmost care, still if you have any suggestions regarding its improvement, then feel free to contact us at olympiads@bloomcap.org. We will try to inculcate your suggestions in the further editions.

Contents

Odd and Even Numbers

1. There are some students standing with balloons in their hand as show in below diagram. The number written on the balloons is the cost of it.

Who is holding a balloon of odd costing?

(a) Sonal

(b) Suman

(c) Vanshika

(d) Rohit

2. Which of the following set of numbers are arranged in decreasing order?

(a) 371, 379, 397, 378

(b) 378, 371, 397, 379

(b) 397, 379, 378, 371

(d) 379, 397, 378, 371

3. The life span of four animals is given below:

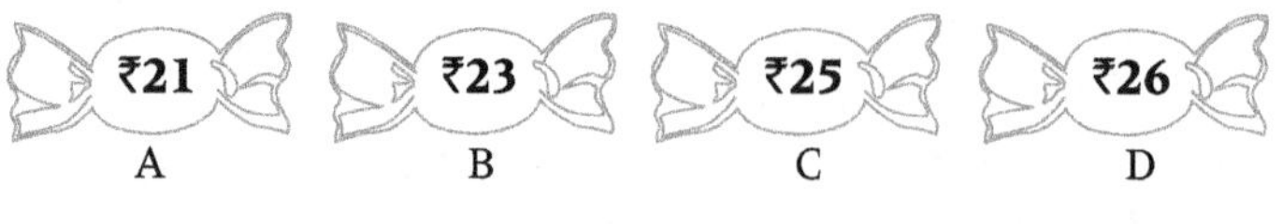

Animal	Tortoise	Elephant	Lion	Chicken
Life span (in years)	193	70	35	15

Which of the following animals lives for an even number of years?
(a) Tortoise   (b) Elephant   (c) Lion   (d) Chicken

4. There are given some candies with their costs. Find out which candies's cost is in an even number?

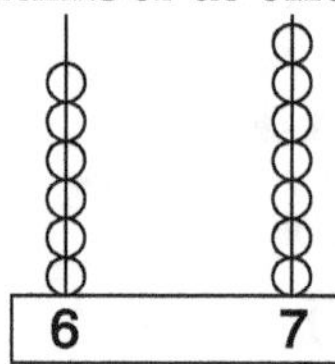

(a) B   (b) C   (c) D   (d) A

5. Ruchika bought an Olympiad book. The cost of the book is obtained by interchanging the 1st and the 3rd digits of the number 942. What is the cost of the book?
(a) ₹ 429   (b) ₹ 249   (c) ₹ 924   (d) ₹ 429

6. Anubhav saw an abacus with a number as shown below:

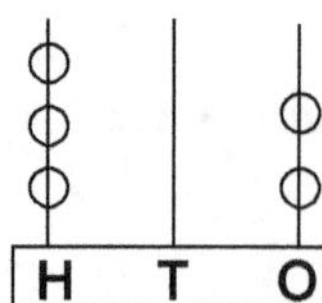

Identify the place of 7.
(a) Ones   (b) Tens   (c) Hundred   (d) Thousand

7. What is the place value of 9 in the largest 3-digit number?
(a) Ones   (b) Tens   (c) Hundreds   (d) All of these

8. Anu has 5 beads. She arranged the beads in the following manner.

How many beads must be placed at tens place to make the number as small as possible?
(a) 2 beads   (b) 3 beads   (c) 1 bead   (d) No beads

9. An old man had a farm of carrots. He planted some carrots in the farm. The number of carrots planted by him is more than 420

   Which of the following cannot be the number of carrots planted by old man?

   (a) 684   (b) 389   (c) 589   (d) 784

10. Nikhil, has lost his puppy. Each puppy given in the options has a number written on it. Use the clues to find his puppy.

    Clue 1 The number at tens place is double the number at ones place.

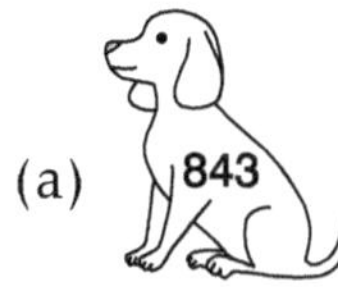

(a)

(b)

(c)

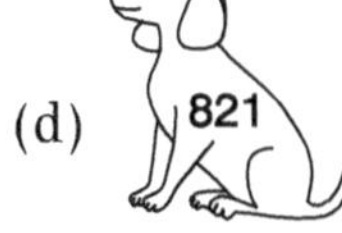

(d)

11. Maria is reading a book. The book has pages more than one hundred sixty five but less than one hundred eighty.

Name of book	Number of pages
Blue fairy	100 + 70 + 0
Snow white	100 + 7 + 10
Cinder	100 + 60
Puss in boots	70 + 10 + 0

Which book is Maria reading?

(a) Blue fairy   (b) Snow white   (c) Cinder   (d) Puss in boots

12. The given diagram shows the number of carrots eaten by each rabbit in a month.

Carrots more than two hundred and 6 is in its ten's place.

(a) Both Bunny and Coco   (b) Piglu
(c) Fluffy   (d) Both Ginger and Fluffy

13. The table below shows the number of pencils four shopkeepers have.

Shopkeepers	Number of Pencils
Anand stationers	15 tens + 3 ones
Curiosity stationers	2 hundreds + 11 tens + 5 ones
JK stationers	51 tens + 3 ones + 0 ones
Array's stationers	3 hundreds + 51 ones

Which of the following is correct?

(a) JK stationers has 154 pencils.

(b) Array's stationers has 381 pencils.

(c) Curiosity stationers has 315 pencils.

(d) Anand stationers has 593 pencils.

14. Which of the following has the largest value?

 (a) Sixty nine

 (b) 7 more than 61

 (c) 5 less than 67

 (d) Even number after sixty five

15. Which of the following is incorrect?

 (a) $327 > 317$

 (b) $467 < 476$

 (c) Fifty seven > fifty three

 (d) $627 > 9$ more than 661

16. The table below shows the number of newspapers sold on different days

Days	Number of Newspapers
Monday	623
Tuesday	482
Wednesday	497
Thursday	625
Friday	452

Which of the following statement is/are correct?

(a) The number of newspapers sold on Tuesday is more than the number of newspapers sold on Wednesday.

(b) The number of newspapers sold on Thursday is highest.

(c) The number of newspapers sold on Friday is smallest.

(d) Both (b) and (c)

17. Compare and fill the boxes using $<$, $>$ or $=$.

 A. 2 tens 3 ones ☐ 53 ones.

 B. Two hundred and two ☐ one hundred and two.

 C. $200 + 60 + 3$ ☐ $200 + 70$

 D. 72 tens ☐ $700 + 20 + 0$

	A	B	C	D			A	B	C	D
(a)	$<$	$>$	$<$	$=$		(b)	$<$	$>$	$=$	$=$
(c)	$>$	$>$	$<$	$=$		(d)	$<$	$>$	$<$	$<$

18. Chiku, found some lost pages of his book. Help him to arrange them in the correct order.

(a) 15, 84, 49, 65   (b) 49, 15, 65, 84   (c) 84, 65, 49, 15   (d) 15, 49, 65, 84

19. Write the descending order of the given collection of numbers.

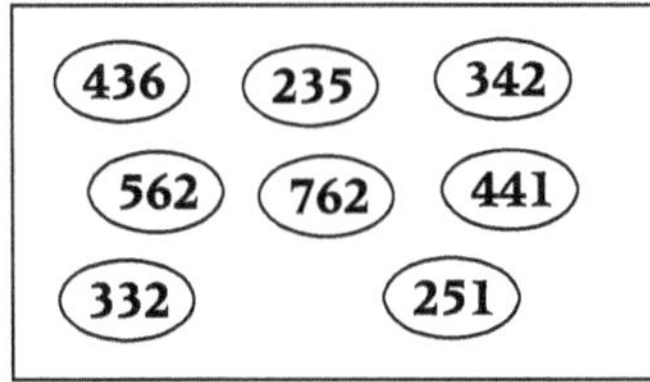

(a) 762 > 562 > 441 > 436 > 342 > 332 > 251 > 235
(b) 762 > 562 > 441 > 342 > 436 > 332 > 251 > 235
(c) 762 > 441 > 342 > 562 > 436 > 332 > 251 > 235
(d) 762 > 562 > 441 > 436 > 342 > 235 > 251 > 332

20. Khushboo has the set of number cards 8 6 4. Which is the smallest possible 3-digit number that can be formed by using each card only once?

(a) 648   (b) 468   (c) 864   (d) 486

Directions (Q. Nos. 21 and 22) The train given below shows the number of passengers in each compartment.

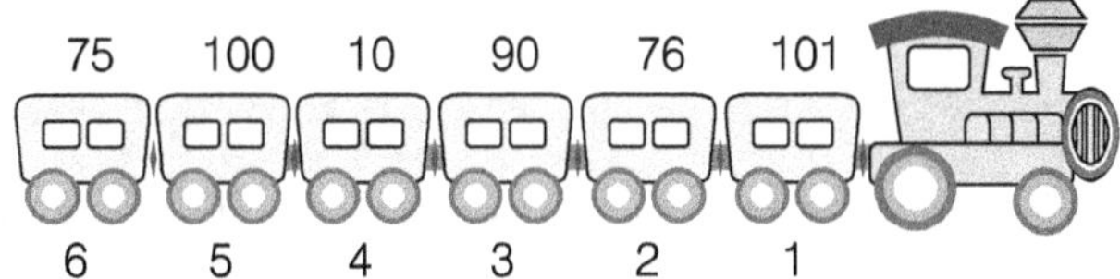

21. The .... compartment has 75 passengers.

(a) fifth   (b) second   (c) third   (d) sixth

22. Which compartment has the number of passengers equal to the smallest 3-digit number?

(a) First   (b) Fourth   (c) Fifth   (d) Third

23. State 'T' for true and 'F' for false.

1. There are 0 ones in 406.
2. The number 99 is just before the smallest 3-digit number.
3. 800 ones is same as 80 tens.
4. The largest 3-digit number formed using the digits 9, 2, 5 is an odd number.

	1	2	3	4
(a)	F	F	F	T
(b)	F	T	T	F
(c)	F	F	T	T
(d)	T	F	T	F

Chapter 02

Addition and Subtraction

1. Add the three digit number $342 + 124$

    (a) 466   (b) 584   (c) 324   (d) 259

2. Add the two digit number $49 + 36$

    (a) 80   (b) 85   (c) 75   (d) 65

3. This is a machine which takes input and gives output as shown in the figure.

What input should be provided in the machine, so that the output is 460?

    (a) 208, 295   (b) 196, 264

    (c) 156, 178   (d) 352, 109

4. The given table shows the number of hours, Vinay watched TV on different days.

Days	Hours
Monday	X X X
Tuesday	X X
Wednesday	X X X X
Thursday	X X
Friday	X X
Saturday	X X X X X
Sunday	–

$X \rightarrow$ Represents $\rightarrow$ 1 Hour.

How many hours does Vinay watch TV in a week?

    (a) 10   (b) 18

    (c) 11   (d) 14

5. A rainbow is seen in rainy season. It consists of seven different colours.

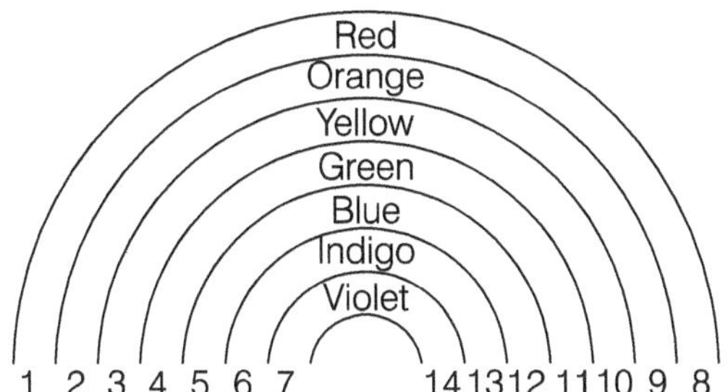

   Which colour of the rainbow has the number whose sum is second lowest?
   (a) Red   (b) Orange   (c) Violet   (d) Indigo

6. Raju has ₹ 24 in his one pocket and ₹ 39 in another pocket. What total amount of money does Raju has?
   (a) ₹ 63   (b) ₹ 36   (c) ₹ 69   (d) ₹ 72

7. Anjali bought 167 pencils on Friday, 234 pencils on Sunday and 371 pencils on Tuesday. How many pencils did she buy in all?
   (a) 727   (b) 691   (c) 792   (d) 772

8. Study the given pattern very carefully.

	485				923				?	
240	130	115		105	382	436		195	218	533

   Find the missing number.
   (a) 983   (b) 905   (c) 994   (d) 946

9. Kartik is reading a story book that has 87 pages. To complete the book, Kartik has to read 24 more pages. How many has kartik read so far?
   (a) 61   (b) 56   (c) 63   (d) 68

10. Subtract the given 3-digit numbers: 889 – 267
    (a) 572   (b) 652   (c) 622   (d) 782

11. Subtract the given 2-digit number : 75 – 27
    (a) 47   (b) 46   (c) 45   (d) 48

12. Find the value of

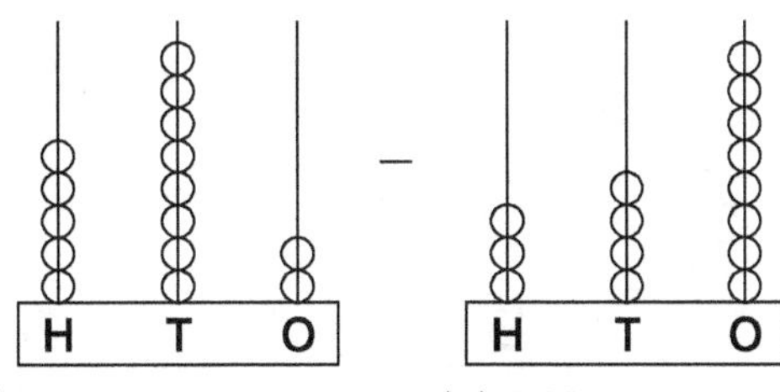

    (a) 384   (b) 843   (c) 348   (d) 234

13. There were 927 passengers in a train. At first station 369 passengers deboard the train. How many passengers remaining now in train?
(a) 578   (b) 558   (c) 672   (d) 498

14. Difference between the largest 3-digit odd number and the smallest 3-digit number?
(a) 797   (b) 899   (c) 897   (d) 799

15. George has 9 pencils.

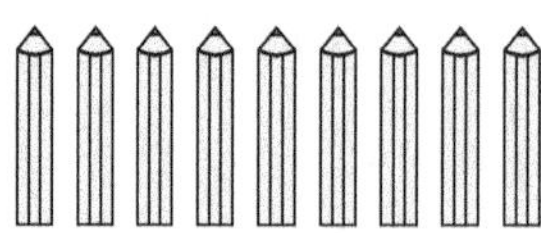

He distributed all the pencils among his sisters. If each of his sister got 3 pencils. then, how many sisters does George have?
(a) 2   (b) 3   (c) 4   (d) 1

16. Study the given pattern very carefully and find the missing number.

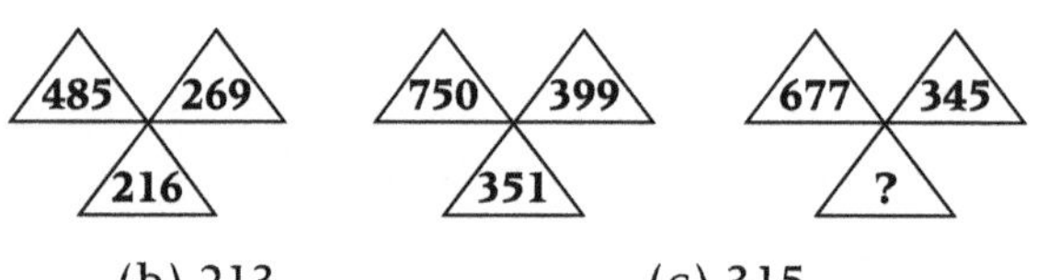

(a) 332   (b) 213   (c) 315   (d) 460

Directions (Q.Nos. 17 and 18) Study the table carefully and answer the following questions.

Classroom	Number of benches
6	32
7	37
8	29
9	46

17. What is the total number of benches in classroom 7 and 9 ?
(a) 38   (b) 78   (c) 81   (d) 83

18. Classroom 8 has how many benches less than classroom 7?
(a) 9   (b) 8   (c) 10   (d) 6

19. Which of the following statement is incorrect?
(a) $150 + 245 = 395$ (b) $500 - 105 = 395$
(c) $195 + 200 = 395$ (d) $1000 - 505 = 395$

20. Which two sets of values are equal?

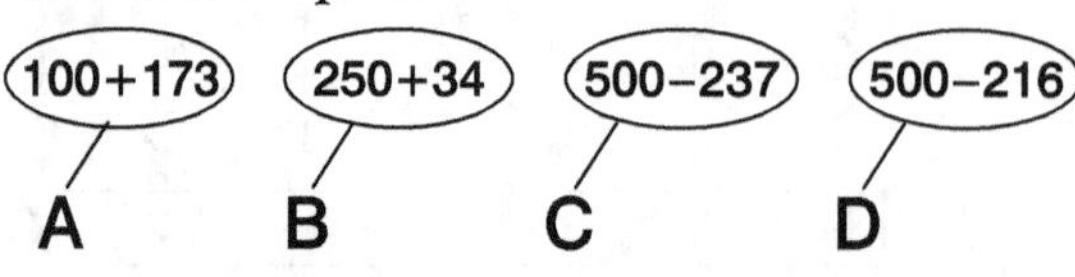

(a) A and B   (b) B and D   (c) B and C   (d) D and A

21. If the value of $\triangle$ = 49 and $\square$ = 38.

What is the value of $\triangle + \triangle - \square$ =?

(a) 60   (b) 68   (c) 57   (d) 51

22. Richa has three numbers

What is the maximum result she can get by adding any two numbers and then subtracting the third number from it?

(a) 10   (b) 6   (c) 2   (d) 12

23. The sum of the numbers on the school bag is

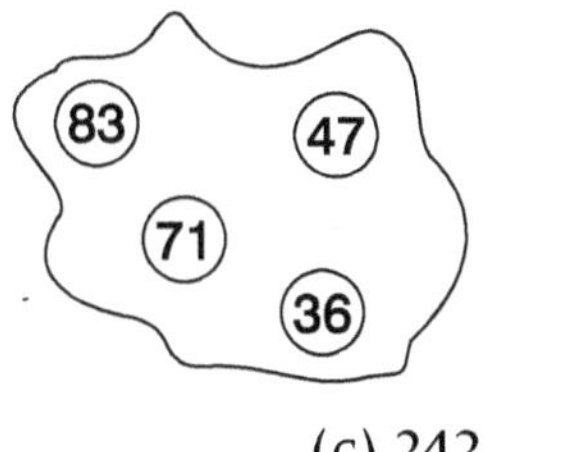

(a) 231   (b) 237   (c) 242   (d) 227

24. A number machine takes any number put into it, add 15, then subtract 9, then add 37 and then subtract 20.

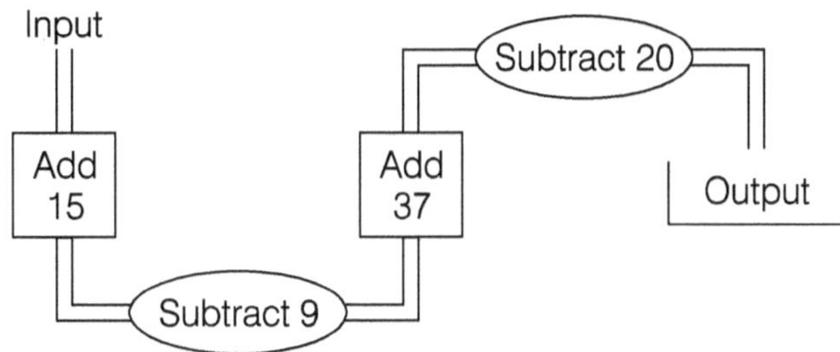

If 21 is put into machine, what number comes out from it?

(a) 39   (b) 42   (c) 44   (d) 43

25. Rishu is thinking of a number. He challenges his friend to find the number.

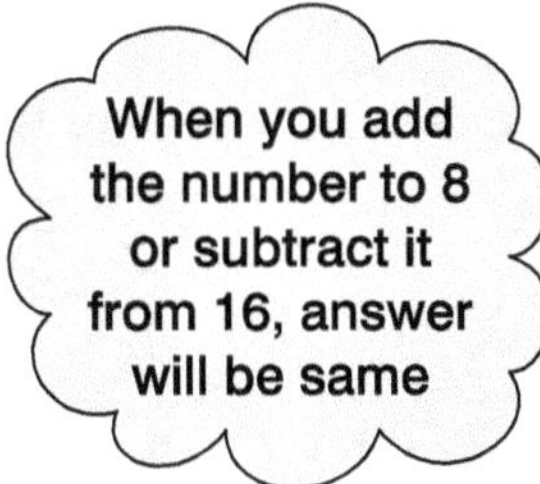

The number is

(a) 6   (b) 5   (c) 8   (d) 4

Multiplication

1. Which number should come in place of question mark?

   $0 \times 1 \times 2 = ?$

   (a) 7   (b) 8   (c) 0   (d) 9

2. Which two multiplication sentences does the given figure represents?

   (a) $4 \times 2, 2 \times 4$ (b) $3 \times 2, 2 \times 3$

   (c) $4 \times 3, 3 \times 4$ (d) None of these

3. If 9 players in a cricket match score 30 runs each. How many runs were scored?

   (a) 270   (b) 210

   (c) 250   (d) 230

4. One pentagon has 5 sides. How many sides will 5 pentagon have?

   (a) 19   (b) 26

   (c) 20   (d) 25

5. How many jumps does the frog need to make to reach his tadpole?

   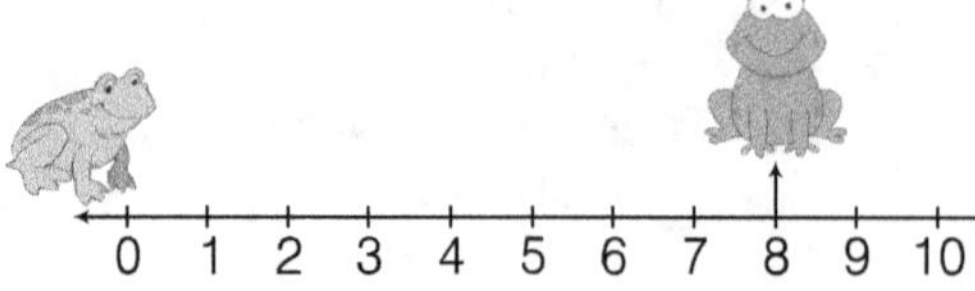

   (a) 4 jumps of 2   (b) 2 jumps of 4

   (c) 1 jump of 8   (d) Either (a), (b) or (c)

6. Find the total money if you have 7 notes of ₹ 50.

    (a) ₹ 350   (b) ₹ 300   (c) ₹ 400   (d) ₹ 250

7. How many pairs of legs does 8 spiders have?

    (a) 64   (b) 8   (c) 56   (d) 32

8. There are 18 apples hanging on each tree. How many apples are there on 9 trees?

    (a) 144   (b) 162   (c) 188   (d) 172

9. There are 24 boys and 36 girls in each class. How many students are there in 8 classes?

    (a) 450   (b) 490   (c) 480   (d) 360

10. Match the following and choose the correct option.

1. .... $\times 5 = 40$	A.	4
2. $934 \times .... = 934$	B.	8
3. 2 times of the smallest even number = ...	C.	90
4. $9 \times 10 = ...$	D.	1

Codes

	1	2	3	4
(a)	C	A	B	D
(b)	B	D	C	A
(c)	A	C	B	D
(d)	B	D	A	C

11. Fill in the blanks.

A. 8	B. 20
C. 7	D. 35
E. 32	F. 16
G. 500	H. 0
I. 5	

1. There are ____ 7's in 35.

2. 25 tens $\times$ 2 ones = ____

3. There are 4 children in a class. Each children ate 5 toffees. They ate ____ toffees in all.

4. 8 groups of 4 is equal to ....

Codes

	1	2	3	4
(a)	C	I	B	A
(b)	I	G	B	E
(c)	I	H	F	A
(d)	C	G	F	E

12. The following diagram shows the way of Misha's house and a nearby park

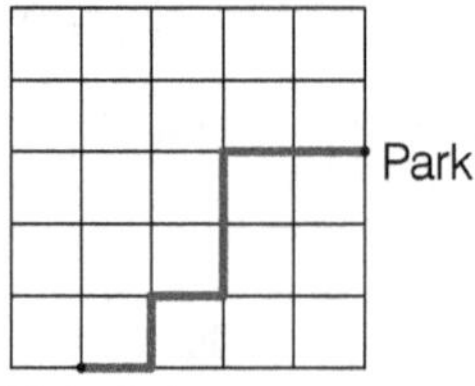

If each ▭ = 3 steps, then how many steps will Misha move in order to reach park from her house?

(a) 21   (b) 24   (c) 18   (d) 7

13. Given grid consists of numbers in rows and columns.

	7	8
3	A	B
4	C	D

Find A, B, C and D by multiplying the numbers.

	A	B	C	D
(a)	24	28	32	21
(b)	9	16	49	64
(c)	21	24	28	32
(d)	16	9	64	49

14. Identify the given diagram very carefully.

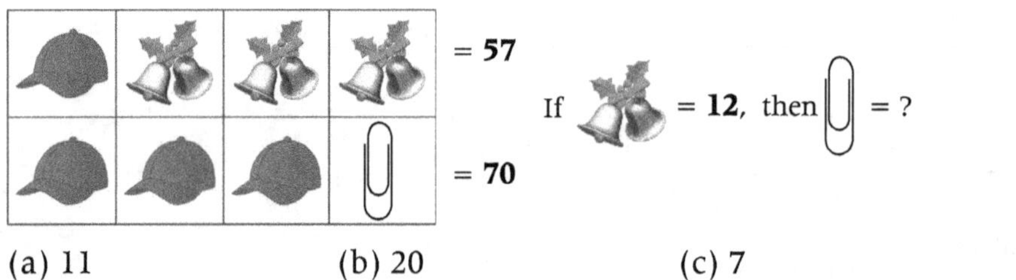

(a) 11   (b) 20   (c) 7   (d) 21

15. Mary stays on the thirteenth floor of an apartment. The number of steps on each staircase is given. How many steps on the staircases does Mary have to climb to reach her floor?

(a) 104   (b) 84   (c) 81   (d) 102

16. What would be the total cost of 4 kg of guava at the rate of ₹ 40 per kg and 3 kg of mangoes at the rate of ₹ 25 per kg?
    (a) ₹ 220   (b) ₹ 250
    (c) ₹ 235   (d) ₹ 275

17. Salia bought 4 dozen of trays from the market. Out of them, 5 were defective and 15 broke down. How many good trays are there? (1 dozen = 12units)
    (a) 33   (b) 43
    (c) 30   (d) 28

18. There are 4 groups of girls in the hall. There are 6 girls in each group. Three minutes later, 6 girls walk into the hall and join them. How many girls are there in the hall now?
    (a) 30   (b) 35
    (c) 28   (d) 25

19. On saturday in 7 sections of class 5, 30 boys were absent from total number of boys in all section of class 5. If in each section number of boys is 15, then how many boys were present on saturday?
    (a) 70   (b) 65
    (c) 75   (d) None of these

20. A shopkeeper sold thrice as many kinder joy on Sunday than on saturday and he sold 4 times as many kinder joy on Wednesday than on Sunday. He sold 20 kinder joy on Saturday. How many kinder joy did he sell Sunday and Wednesday both respectively.
    (a) 200   (b) 300
    (c) 150   (d) 250

Division

1. Find the number which divided by 7 gives 5 as a remainder and 2 as the quotient.
   (a) 18   (b) 12
   (c) 36   (d) 19

2. Find the missing number in the following pattern

21	12	18	?
7	4	6	5

   (a) 15   (b) 14   (c) 18   (d) 24

3. Mrs. Bhaskar's music school has 48 children. She has divided the children into 6 equal groups. How many children are in each group?
   (a) $48 + 6 = 54$ (b) $8 \times 6 = 48$
   (c) $48 - 8 = 40$ (d) $48 \div 6 = 8$

4. If ☆ ☆ ☆ stands for 12 stickers. How many stickers does ☆ ☆ ☆ ☆ ☆ stands?
   (a) 12   (b) 24
   (c) 16   (d) 20

5. How many bananas every child will get if the given number of bananas is equally divided among 3 children?

   (a) 5   (b) 3   (c) 4   (d) 6

6. Virat has 12 pencils.

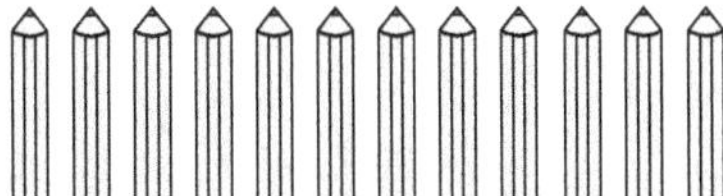

   He distributed all the pencils among his sisters. If each of his sister got 3 pencils. Then, how many sisters does virat have?

   (a) 2   (b) 3   (c) 4   (d) 1

7. A bucket has 54 L of water Capacity.

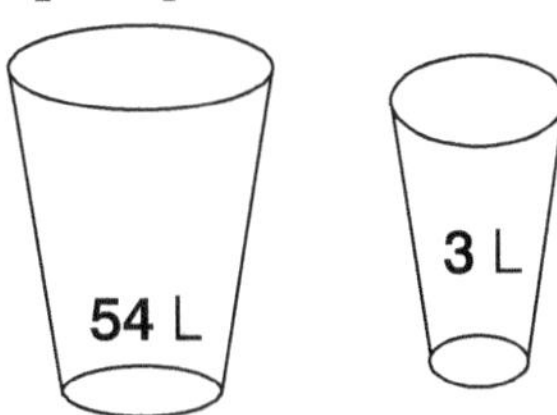

   How many glasses of water can it be poured into bucket, so that bucket will full ?

   (a) 12   (b) 15   (c) 18   (d) 20

8. Tushar has a stand having 2 sticks in it and 8 beads as shown below:

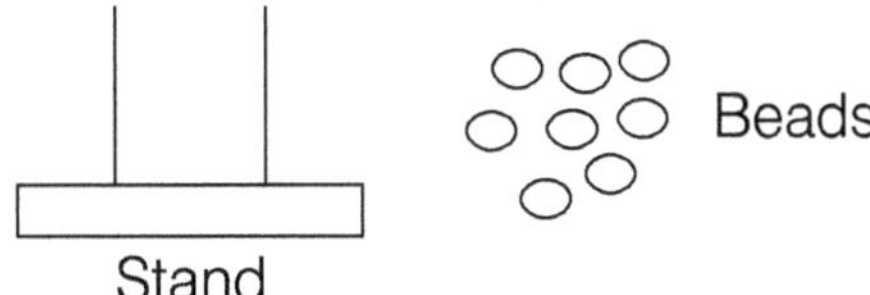

   If Tim divides 8 beads equally between 2 sticks, then how many beads each stick contains?

   (a) 4   (b) 6   (c) 2   (d) 3

9. If 81 chairs is arranged in 9 rows, find the total number of each row?

   (a) 8   (b) 9   (c) 10   (d) 15

10. Kareena has only 7 days to read a book. The book consist 52 pages. How many pages left to be read?

    (a) 4   (b) 3   (c) 7   (d) 8

11. 24 girls and 21 boys went for a picnic. They formed 5 equal groups. How many children were there in each group?

    (a) 8   (b) 9   (c) 12   (d) 10

12. 21 chocolates are distributed among 7 boys equally. Then, how many chocolates 4 boys will get ?

    (a) 12   (b) 14   (c) 18   (d) 9

13. Akshay has 72 chocolates. He wants to distribute them in his 4 friends. How many chocolates each friend will get?

    (a) 18   (b) 12   (c) 16   (d) 14

14. Laxman bought candles in pack of five. He has 30 candles in all. How many packs of candles did he buy?

    (a) 6   (b) 8   (c) 5   (d) 7

15. Some glasses of shikanji were bought for ₹ 64 and 8 friends share the bill equally. What is the share of each?

    (a) ₹ 7   (b) ₹ 8

    (c) ₹ 6   (d) ₹ 12

16. Gaurav and two of his friends want to pack 36 gifts for their classmates. The three of them want to pack equal number of gifts. How many gifts should each one pack?

    (a) 14   (b) 16

    (c) 25   (d) 12

17. Ruby had 42 number of mangoes. 9 mangoes were rotten. She kept the rest equally in some bags. How many bags did Ruby use, if each bag had 3 mangoes?

    (a) 12   (b) 14

    (c) 11   (d) 13

18. Akansha has 36 toy cars. She arrange them in rows of 6. How many more toy cars does she need, if she wants to have 8 such rows?

    (a) 8   (b) 42

    (c) 14   (d) 12

19. State 'T' for true and 'F' for false.

    1. Any number divided by the number itself gives 0.

    2. Any number divided by 1 gives the number itself.

    3. If the cost of 2 tables is ₹400, then the cost of 1 table is ₹190.

    4. The number that we are dividing by is called dividend.

	1	2	3	4			1	2	3	4
(a)	F	T	F	F		(b)	T	F	T	F
(c)	F	F	T	F		(d)	F	T	T	F

Measurement

1. The measurements on the given scale got disappeared. Which of the following can be length of the scale?

(a) 8 centimetres
(b) 7 centimetres
(c) 9 centimetres
(d) 10 centimetres

2. What is the length of the cassette, which is given below?

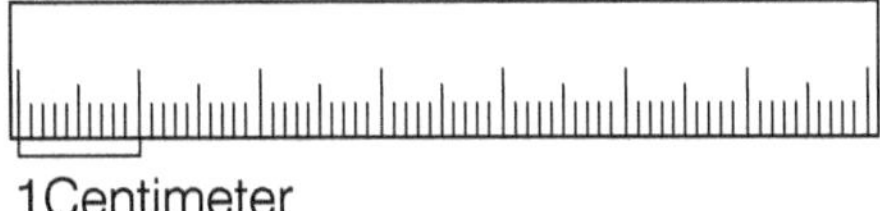

(a) 4 inches
(b) 5 inches
(c) 6 inches
(d) 10 inches

3. Sunil is at Delhi and want to go Jaipur. Observe the diagram given below:

What is the distance between Delhi and Jaipur?
(a) 599 kilometers
(b) 549 kilometers
(c) 373 kilometers
(d) 432 kilometers

18

4. The diagram shown below is a racing track.

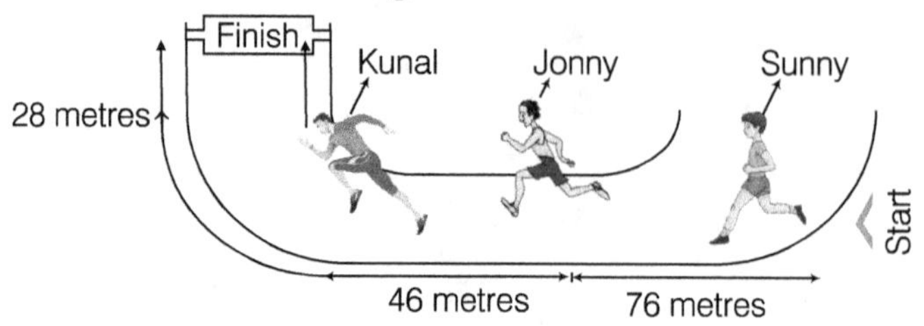

How much distance does Sunny needs to run in order to win?
(a) 104 metres
(b) 74 metres
(c) 125 metres
(d) 150 metres

5. Monku, a monkey likes to eat coconut. The coconut tree is 43 metres high. Monku is sitting on a wooden block whose height is 15 metres. How much high does Monku need to jump to reach coconut?

(a) 28 metres
(b) 32 metres
(c) 58 metres
(d) 40 metres

6. Ronnie joined 5 pieces of rope to form a larger rope. The length of each piece is 12 centimetres. How long was the larger rope formed?
(a) 72 centimetres
(b) 65 centimetres
(c) 60 centimetres
(d) 12 centimetres

7. What is the length of the longest pencil?

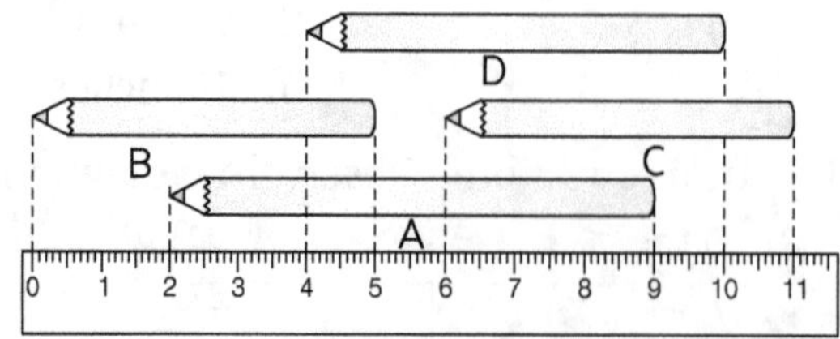

(a) 9 centimetres
(b) 7 centimetres
(c) 11 centimetres
(d) 6 centimetres

8. Study the diagram given below:

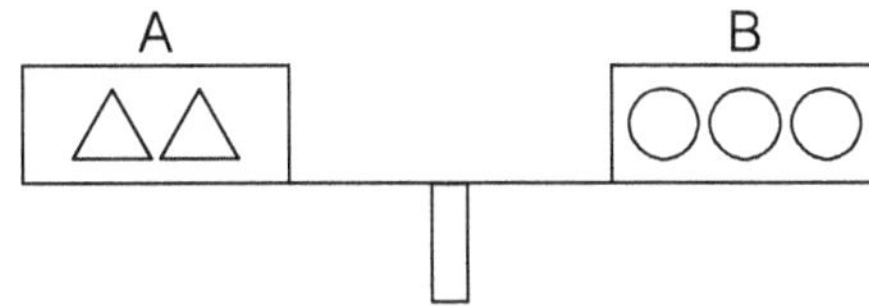

$\Delta = 4$ kg, $O = 3$ kg

Which box is heavy?

(a) A
(b) B
(c) Both are equal
(d) Cannot be determined

9. The weight of Zoya holding a puppy is as shown below.

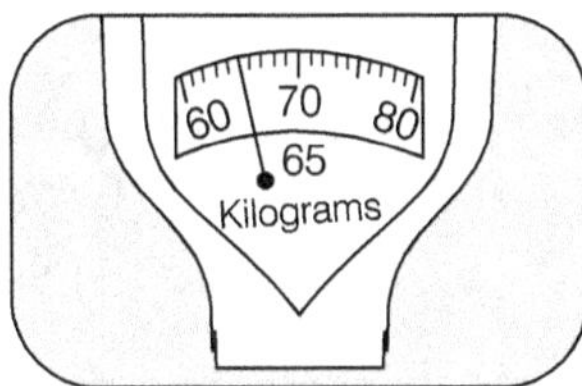

If the weight of the puppy is 4 kilograms. Then, what is the weight of Zoya?

(a) 64 kilograms
(b) 65 kilograms
(c) 61 kilograms
(d) 63 kilograms

10. If each $O = 7$ grams, then the mass of the box is ....

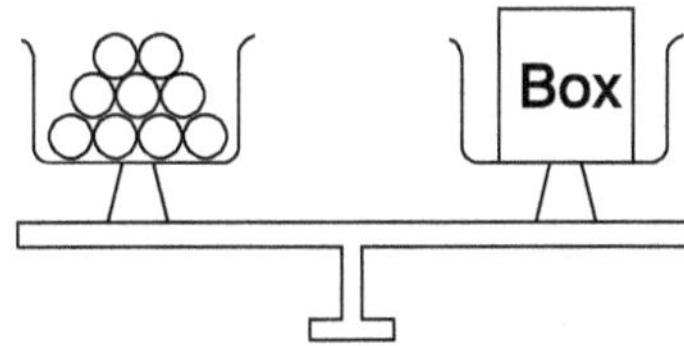

(a) 56 grams
(b) 63 grams
(c) 42 grams
(d) None of these

11. Adira is 10 kilograms heavier than Beth. Beth is 7 kilograms lighter than Saira. Saira is 35 kilograms. What is the weight of Adira?

(a) 35 kilograms
(b) 28 kilograms
(c) 38 kilograms
(d) 45 kilograms

12. Find the weight of the Mango?

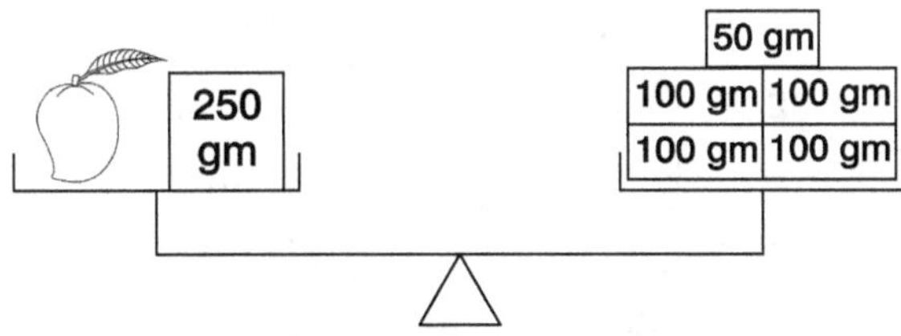

(a) 150 gm
(b) 250 gm
(c) 300 gm
(d) 200 gm

Directions (Q. Nos. 13 and 14) Observe the weight of each fruit and answer the following questions.

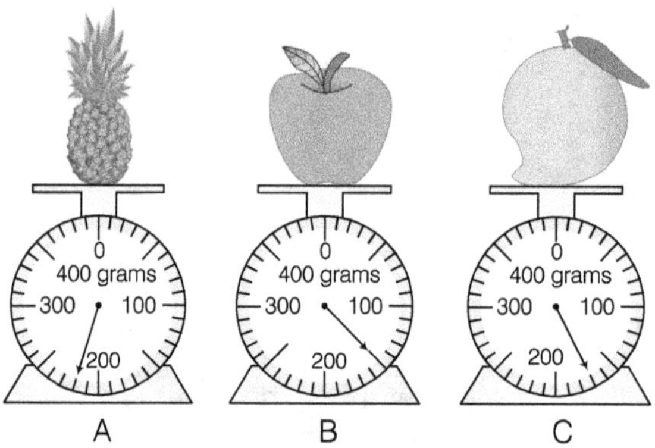

13. What is the difference between the weight of a pineapple and a mango?
    (a) 100 grams
    (b) 70 grams
    (c) 30 grams
    (d) 50 grams

14. If a mango is also placed on machine B, then which of the following statement is correct?
    (a) Weight on machine A is greatest.
    (b) Weight on machine C is least.
    (c) Weight on machine B is greatest.
    (d) Both (b) and (c).

15. Which of the following container holds the greatest quantity of water?
    [**Hint** 100 ml = 1 litre]

(A) 

11 Litres

(B) 

12 Litres and
726 millilitres

(C) 

9 Litres and
100 millilitres

(D 

8 Litres and
345 millilitres

    (a) A
    (b) B
    (c) C
    (d) D

16. A factory requires the following amount of water each day:

Days	Volume
Monday	150 litres
Tuesday	243 litres
Wednesday	182 litres

How much total volume of water does the factory requires in all the three days?

(a) 425 litres   (b) 575 litres   (c) 332 litres   (d) 675 litres

17. If you drink 3 litres of water per day, then how much water will you drink in 2 weeks?

(a) 21 litres   (b) 42 litres   (c) 63 litres   (d) 35 litres

18. Prachi has given a task of filling up the tank using bucket. The volume of tank is 45 litres. The volume of the bucket is 5 litres. How many buckets are required by Prachi to fill the tank completely?

(a) 7   (b) 8   (c) 9   (d) 10

19. Greta's mother is ill. Greta has to do all the household work.

The volume of water required by Greta and her mother in their work is as follows.

Household work	Greta	Greta's mother
Cooking	15 litres	10 litres
Cleaning	50 litres	40 litres
Washing clothes	40 litres	30 litres

How much extra water is used by Greta in all the household work, then her mother?

(a) 28 litres   (b) 30 litres   (c) 50 litres   (d) 25 litres

20. If the temperature in thermometer is 67°C and the room temerature is 19°C less than the temperature in thermometer, then what is the room temperature?

(a) 40°C   (b) 38°C   (c) 35°C   (d) 48°C

21. Match the following and mark the correct option.

1. Sugar   A. 2 metres   3. Beaker   C. 300 millilitres

2. Door   B. 20 kilograms   4. Glass   D. 7 litres

	1	2	3	4
(a)	B	C	A	D
(b)	D	B	C	A
(c)	C	D	B	A
(d)	B	A	D	C

Money

1. ☐ 25 paise coins = 1 rupee

   Which number should come in box?

   (a) 4 (b) 8 (c) 7 (d) 6

2. Lero wants to play a game. The machine accepts only paise. So, Lero changes the given amount to paise.

   How much paise did he receive for playing the game?

   (a) 575 paise (b) 650 paise (c) 600 paise (d) 675 paise

3. A juice machine charges ₹ 65 for a can of juice. The machine requires exact change. Which of the following combination of coins and notes should be put in?

   (a)    

   (b)  

   (c)   

   (d) 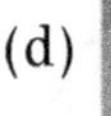   

4. The picture below shows the savings of four children.

Match each child with the amount of money he/she has.

1. Kate		A. ₹ 50
2. Zeena		B. ₹ 30
3. Amira		C. ₹ 60
4. Brad		D. ₹ 40

	1	2	3	4			1	2	3	4
(a)	D	C	B	A		(b)	D	B	A	C
(c)	C	B	A	D		(d)	C	D	B	A

5. Which of the following shows the greatest amount?

(a)   (b)

(c)   (d) None of the above

6. Arrange the given items from the most expensive to the most cheapest.

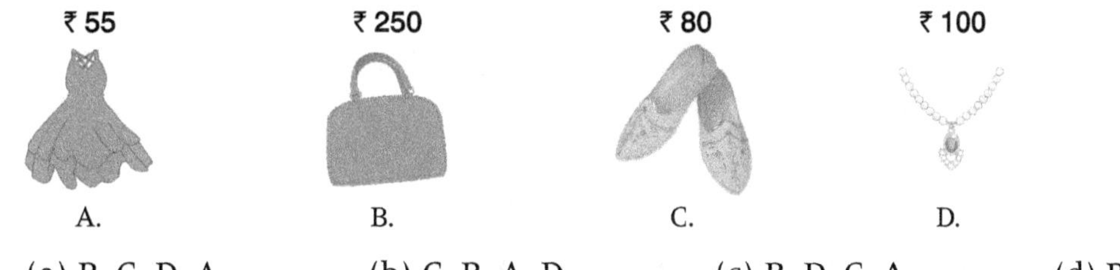

(a) B, C, D, A   (b) C, B, A, D   (c) B, D, C, A   (d) B, C, D, A

7. Sushil bought a pencil box and a book. The pencil box costs ₹ 20 and book cost is ₹ 32.50. How much did he pay altogether?

(a) ₹ 50   (b) ₹ 42.50   (c) ₹ 52.00   (d) ₹ 52.50

8. Sonam wants to buy some chocolates. The cost of 3 chocolates is ₹ 10. How many chocolates can she buy with ₹ 30?

   (a) 3   (b) 6

   (c) 9   (d) 12

9. Given below is the price list of 4 items sold in a bookshop.

Pencil	Sharpener	Eraser	Ruler
30 paise	50 paise	45 paise	35 paise

   Greta has 85 paise with her. Which two items can she buy with all the amount she has?

   (a) A sharpener and an eraser   (b) A pencil and a ruler

   (c) A sharpner and a ruler   (d) An eraser and a ruler

10. Kaira bought a purse whose cost is ₹ 450. She received ₹ 235 change. How much money she paid?

    (a) ₹ 658   (b) ₹ 700

    (c) ₹ 685   (d) ₹ 695

11. Prabhat has ₹ 12.75. He bought a chocolate for ₹ 5. How much money with him is remaining?

    (a) ₹ 5.50   (b) ₹ 7.75

    (c) ₹ 4.25   (d) ₹ 7.50

12. Simone buys of a hamburger and a cookie for ₹ 28 and ₹ 45, respectively. Simone has a coupon of ₹ 10. How much money does Simone have to pay?

    (a) ₹ 60   (b) ₹ 73

    (c) ₹ 85   (d) ₹ 63

13. Jorg had ₹ 524. Yura gave him ₹ 113 more. Jorg gave ₹ 192 to his friend. How much money does Jorg have now?

    (a) ₹ 637   (b) ₹ 445

    (c) ₹ 428   (d) ₹ 692

14. Suzanne had 32 apples. She packed them into packets of 4 and then she sold each packet for ₹ 12 each. How much money would she receive?

    (a) ₹ 108   (b) ₹ 96

    (c) ₹ 84   (d) ₹ 120

15. The cost of a winter cap is ₹ 2 tens and 20 ones. How much money does Ria must have in order to buy the cap?

(a) ₹ 5 tens   (b) ₹ 2 tens and 2 ones

(c) ₹ 3 tens   (d) ₹ 3 tens and 5 ones

16. Corn muffins cost ₹ 2 each. Blueberry muffins cost ₹ 3 each. Which of the following options best describes the total cost of 7 corn muffins and 9 blueberry muffins?

(a) ₹ 39   (b) ₹ 16

(c) ₹ 41   (d) ₹ 21

17. Kim and his family hired a taxi for a picnic. Taxi charges ₹ 15 extra for every hour after 7 : 00 pm. If Kim and his family came home at 12 mid-night, then how much extra money did they had to pay to the driver?

(a) ₹ 65   (b) ₹ 50

(c) ₹ 75   (d) ₹ 80

18. State 'T' for true and 'F' for false.

1. You can exchange five 10 paise coins for one 50 paise coin.
2. You can give four 2 paise coins and one 1 paisa coin to pay 10 paise.
3. Kina has ₹ 35 and Gianne has ₹ 40. They have ₹ 75 in total.
4. If 1 banana cost ₹ 6, then the cost of a dozen of banana is ₹ 72.
   (1 dozen = 12 units)

	1 2 3 4		1 2 3 4		1 2 3 4		1 2 3 4
(a)	T T T F	(b)	T F T T	(c)	T F F T	(d)	F T T F

19. Fill in the blanks.

A. ₹ 75	B. ₹ 82
C. 2	D. ₹ 72
E. 100	F. ₹ 70
G. 4	H. 200
I. 88	

1. There are ____ paise in ₹ 2.
2. ___ 50 paise coins make ₹ 1.
3. ₹ ____ should be added to ₹ 28 to get ₹ 100.
4. If 1 pen costs ₹ 15 and 1 book costs ₹ 55, then the total cost is ₹ ___ .

	1 2 3 4		1 2 3 4
(a)	C B A I	(b)	H C D F
(c)	E G B F	(d)	E G I D

Directions (Q. Nos. 20 and 21) Study the following chart and answer the given questions.

Apples	Strawberries	Bananas	Raspberries	Pineapples	Kiwi fruit
12 paise each	21 paise per kg	18 paise each	34 paise per kg	47 paise each	24 paise each

20. You have been given ₹ 5 to purchase 2 kiwi fruits, 3 kilograms of strawberries and 4 bananas. How much change would you get from the above purchase?
    (a) 500 paise
    (b) 183 paise
    (c) 317 paise
    (d) 247 paise

21. Which of the following is the most expensive purchase?
    (a) 2 kilograms strawberries and a kiwi fruit
    (b) An apple and a pineapple
    (c) 3 bananas and an apple
    (d) 2 kilograms raspberries and a pineapple

22. Mr. and Mrs. Gaston went for a movie. They had a 3 years old boy Misi. Misi had a sister who is 3 years elder and a brother who is 8 years elder than him. How much money they had to pay altogether?

Age group	Amount
Children (below 3)	Free
Adult	₹ 18
Children (above 3 and below 16)	₹ 8

    (a) ₹ 60
    (b) ₹ 52
    (c) ₹ 44
    (d) ₹ 50

Time

1. Kew is reading the clock. She noticed that the hour hand of the clock is between 5 and 6 and the minute hand is at 6. What is the time?
   (a) 5 : 00　　　　　(b) 6 : 00　　　　　(c) 6 : 30　　　　　(d) 5 : 30

2. If the time on the clock is 12 : 30 , then the hour hand is on
   (a) 12　　　　　(b) between 11 and 12　　(c) between 12 and 1　　(d) 1

3. If the arrows represent the hands of the clock, then guess the time.

   (a) 9 : 00 am　　　　　　　　　　(b) 3 : 00 pm
   (c) 3 : 00 am　　　　　　　　　　(d) Either (b) or (c)

4. Identify the correct time. 23 : 30
   (a) 11 : 30 in the morning　　　　　　(b) 11 : 30 in the night
   (c) 10 : 30 in the morning　　　　　　(d) 10 : 30 in the evening

5. How many times in a day does the minute hand is at 12?
   (a) 12　　　　　(b) 24　　　　　(c) 2　　　　　(d) 20

6. 30 seconds + 30 seconds + 30 seconds will be equal to
   (a) 90 seconds　　　　　　　　　　(b) 1 minute 30 seconds
   (c) 2 minutes　　　　　　　　　　(d) both (a) and (b)

7. How many minutes are there in 48 hours?
   (a) 2800 minutes　　　　　　　　　(b) 2600 minutes
   (c) 2880 minutes　　　　　　　　　(d) None of these

8. The diagram shows the feeding time of four cows.

10 minutes   20 minutes   16 minutes   12 minutes

How much time is required to feed all the cows one by one?

(a) 38 minutes   (b) 42 minutes

(c) 56 minutes   (d) 58 minutes

9. The office timing of Kara is from 9 : 00 am to 5 : 00 pm. There is a lunch break for 1 hour. The total working time of Kara is

(a) 7 hours   (b) 8 hours   (c) 6 hours   (d) 10 hours

10. Karen's flight is expected to take off at 4 : 00 pm. The flight takes 2 hours and 20 minutes. At what time the flight will land at its destination?

(a) 5 : 40 pm   (b) 6 : 20 pm

(c) 4 : 40 pm   (d) 7 : 20 pm

11. Elia arrived at the bank at 7 : 10 am. The sign on the door said,

Bank hours : 7 : 30 am to 5 : 00 pm

How long will Elia have to wait for the bank to open?

(a) 20 minutes   (b) 25 minutes   (c) 30 minutes   (d) 15 minutes

12. Tabbu is allowed to watch TV only till 10 : 00 pm. If the time in the evening is as shown in the clock, then for how much more time she can watch TV?

(a) 1 hour   (b) 30 minutes

(c) 1 hour 30 minutes   (d) 2 hours

13. Sara moves the hands of the clock by half an hour and then by 1 hour and repeats the same pattern. In how many turns, the time will be exactly 12 O'clock?

(a) 2   (b) 4   (c) 6   (d) 8

14. In ancient times, hourglasses were used to measure the time. If it takes 30 minutes for sand to come from top to bottom, then calculate the time elapsed, if the hourglass is turned 5 times.

(a) 3 hours   (b) 2 hours 30 minutes   (c) 2 hours   (d) 1 hour 30 minutes

Directions (Q. Nos. 15 and 16) The schedule of three trains is given below:

	Train Names	Departure time from Toledo	Travelling time from Toledo to Blackburn
1.	Simplon-Orient Express	8 : 00 am	6 hours
2.	Eagle Danube Express	8 : 30 am	4:30 hours
3.	Oriental Express	8 : 00 am	5 hours

15. If Lewis wants to reach Blackburn before 1 pm, then which train will he catch?
(a) Simplon-Orient Express   (b) Eagle Danube Express
(c) Oriental Express   (d) None of the above

16. If Oriental Express departs at 9 : 30 am from the platform of Toledo, then at what time will it reach Blackburn?
(a) 2 : 30 pm   (b) 1 : 30 pm   (c) 2 : 00 pm   (d) 3 : 00 pm

17. Alka has a clock whose hour hand has been broken down. Her school finishes off at 3 O' clock in the afternoon. She takes 30 minutes to reach her home. One day she went for having an ice-cream on the way and got late by 10 minutes.

Which of the following could be the time at which Alka reached home?

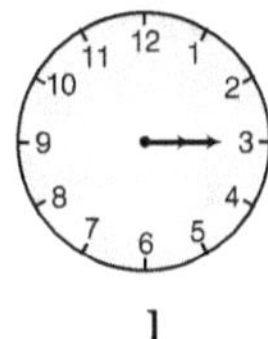   

1   2   3   4

(a) 1   (b) 2   (c) 4   (d) Either 2 or 4

18. Which of the following is correct?
(a) Minute < Hour < Month < Day < Week
(b) Minute < Day < Hour < Week < Month
(c) Minute < Hour < Day < Week < Month
(d) Minute < Hour < Day < Month < Week

19. Kavya was born on 29th February. Her birthday comes

(a) every year

(b) twice in a year

(c) after every four years

(d) after every two years

20. There are 7 days in a week. This year, in the month of February, there are 28 days. The number of days in February is how many times the number of days in a week?

(a) 4 times   (b) 7 times   (c) 21 times   (d) 35 times

Directions (Q. Nos. 21 and 22) Use the following calendar to answer the questions.

March

S	M	T	W	T	F	S
1	2	3	4	5	6	7
8	9	10	11	12	13	14
15	16	17	18	19	20	21
22	23	24	25	26	27	28
29	30	31				

21. How many Sunday are there in the given month?

(a) 5   (b) 4   (c) 6   (d) 3

22. Sara's exams went on for 2 weeks in the month of March commencing from 2nd March and then her vacations started. For how many days did her vacations last in March?

(a) 15 days   (b) 16 days   (c) 17 days   (d) 14 days

23. Study the given calendar and answer the following question.

January

S	M	T	W	T	F	S
				1	2	3
4	5	6	7	8	9	10 World Hindi Day
11	12	13	14	15	16	17
18	19	20	21	22	23	24
25 National Voter's Day	26	27	28	29	30	31

Princy has a test of Mathematics two weeks before National Voter's day. When is her test scheduled?

(a) 14th January

(b) 23rd January

(c) 12th January

(d) 11th January

24. The table below shows the number of days in Some months of a year.

Months	January	February	March
Number of days	31	28	31

What is one way to find total number of days in a year?
(a) multiply 31 by 12   (b) multiply 30 by 12
(c) add the number of days in each month   (d) multiply 31 by 7 and then subtract 28

25. Anu crosses out every fifth day in the given table.

Monday	Tuesday
Wednesday	Thursday
Friday	Saturday
Sunday	Holiday

She started counting from Thursday. After 7 turns, which day will be left without a cross mark?
(a) Friday   (b) Tuesday   (c) Wednesday   (d) Holiday

26. State 'T' for true and 'F' for false.
   1. The shortest hand of the clock is minute hand.
   2. At 6 : 25 the minute hand of the clock is at 5.
   3. 30 minutes after 5 : 30 is 6 : 30.
   4. 1 May 20XX is Sunday. The number of Sunday in this month are 5.

         1 2 3 4   1 2 3 4   1 2 3 4   1 2 3 4
   (a) F T T F   (b) F T T T   (c) F T F T   (d) T F T T

27. Fill in the blanks.

A. July	B. 29
C. Thursday	D. 2
E. 28	F. Friday
G. Wednesday	H. August
I. 1	

   1. 6 tens minutes = _____ hour.
   2. There are _____ days in February in a non-leap year.
   3. If today is Friday, then the day after six days will be _____ .
   4. Seventh month of the year is _______ .

   Codes

         1 2 3 4   1 2 3 4   1 2 3 4   1 2 3 4
   (a) D B H A   (b) D E G C   (c) I E C A   (d) I B C H

Shapes

1. Identify the quadrilateral from the following.

   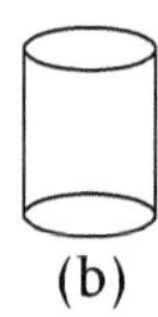   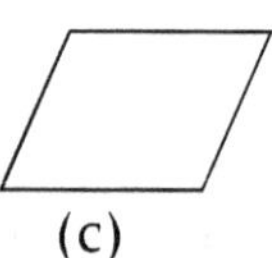   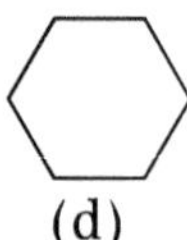

   (a)   (b)   (c)   (d)

2. I have 12 sides and 8 corners. Who am I?

   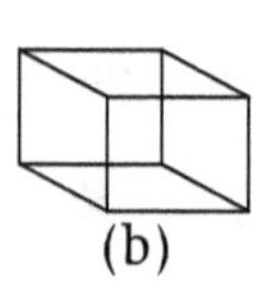   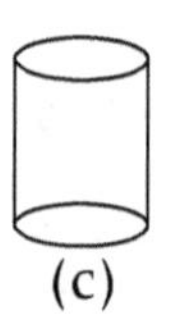   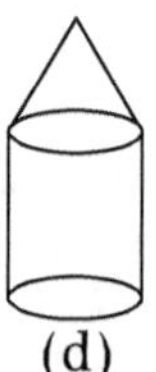

   (a)   (b)   (c)   (d)

3. Which of the given figures consists of the maximum different types of 3-D shapes?

   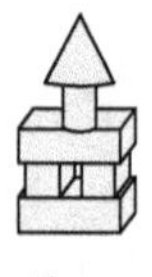   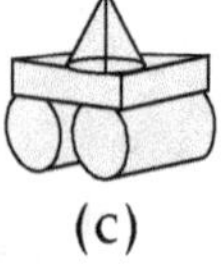   

   (a)   (b)   (c)   (d)

4. The given figure does not consist of ....

(a) rectangle   (b) triangle   (c) square   (d) circle

5. Which of the following figures can be used to draw a circle?

   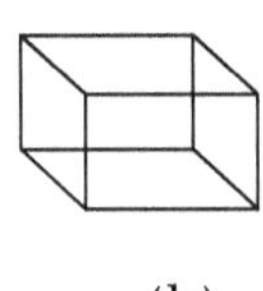   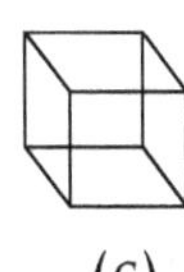   

   (a)   (b)   (c)   (d)

6. The black patch on the football is a

(a) Pentagon   (b) Cone
(c) Square   (d) Circle

7. What is the difference between the number of rectangular faces and square faces in the given solid figure?

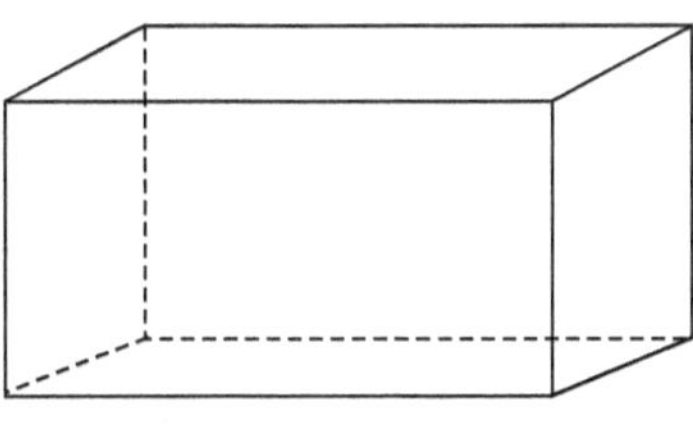

(a) 0   (b) 4
(c) 3   (d) 2

8. Sachin is trying to make the skeleton cube using straws and balls of clay. He uses straws for making edges and clay for making corners.

How many straws and balls of clay will he need?

(a) 8 straws, 6 balls of clay   (b) 8 straws, 12 balls of clay
(c) 12 straws, 6 balls of clay   (d) 12 straws, 8 balls of clay

9. Alisa and her friend have some shapes as given below:

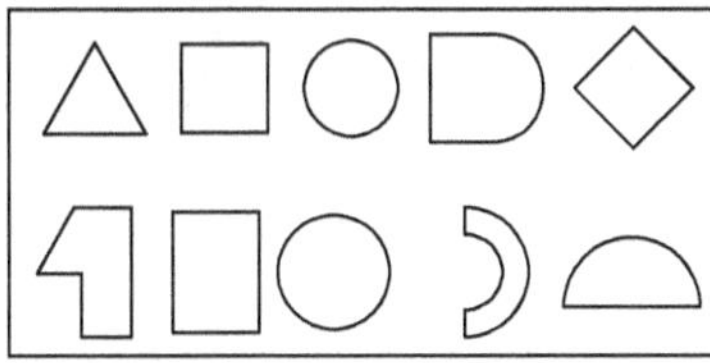

Alisa thought of the shapes that are similar in a certain way as follows

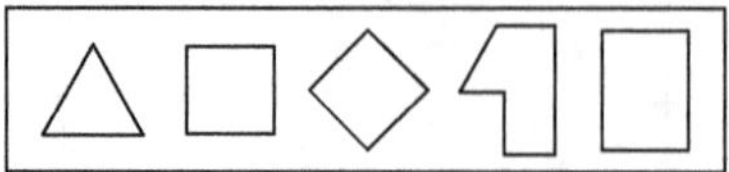

On what basis did Alisa distinguish the given shapes?
(a) The shapes are made up of only four sides
(b) The shapes are made up of only straight lines
(c) The shapes are made up of only curved lines
(d) The shapes are made up of more than four sides

10. How many letters in the given word have only straight lines?

SHAPES

(a) 3   (b) 4   (c) 2   (d) 5

11. Observe the given figure carefully and identify the number of curved lines.

(a) 5   (b) 9   (c) 7   (d) 4

12. Which of the given figures contains 2 straight lines and 2 curved lines?

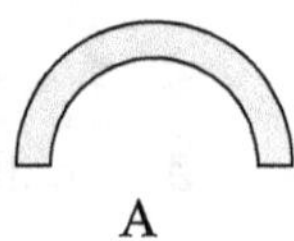

A   B   C   D

(a) A   (b) B   (c) C   (d) D

13. Match the following:

	Figure	Number of straight lines
A.	▭	(1) 5
B.	△	(2) 0
C.	○	(3) 3
D.	⌂	(4) 4

Codes

	A	B	C	D		A	B	C	D		A	B	C	D		A	B	C	D
(a)	3	1	4	2	(b)	4	3	2	1	(c)	2	4	1	3	(d)	3	1	2	4

14. How many squares are used in the given bus?

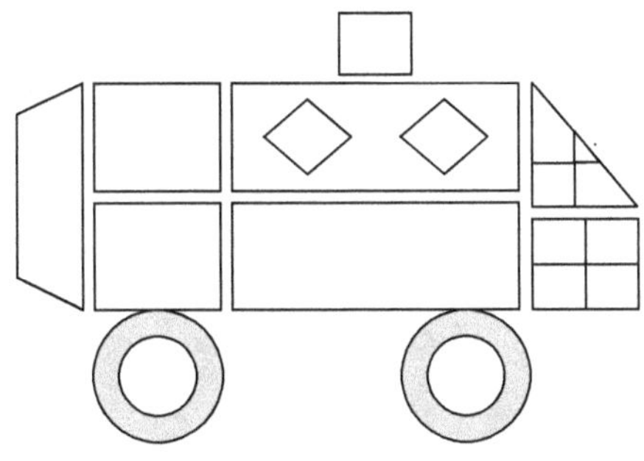

(a) 11   (b) 10   (c) 8   (b) 9

15. Nero saw a flag in the Olympic games.

The number of triangles in the flag is ....
(a) 5   (b) 8   (c) 6   (d) 7

16. Tancy cut-out a square shape into many different shapes as shown below:

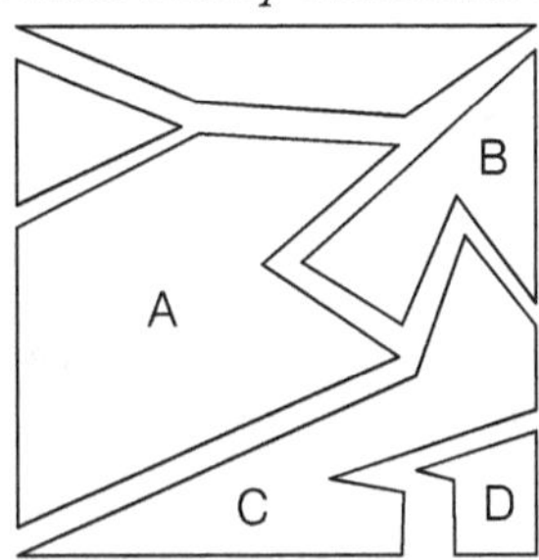

Which shape has the largest number of sides?
(a) A   (b) B   (c) C   (d) D

17. Cyra has 9 toothpicks to make a figure. She uses 6 of the toothpicks as follows:

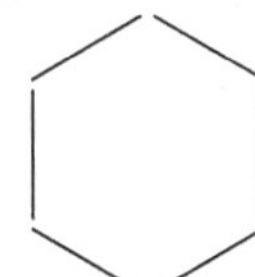

How will she use the remaining toothpicks to divide the above figure into six triangles?

(a) 2 sleeping toothpicks and 1 standing toothpick

(b) 2 slanting toothpicks and 1 standing toothpick

(c) 3 slanting toothpicks

(d) 3 sleeping toothpicks

18. How many more cones are there than the cylinder in the given figure?

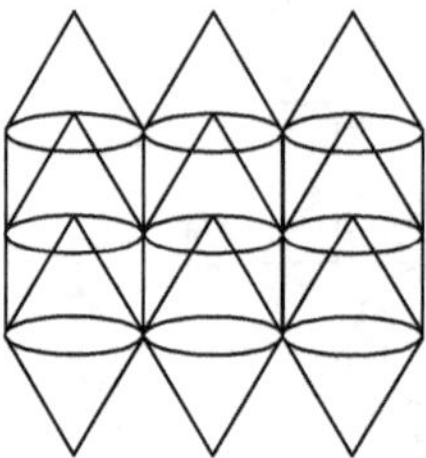

(a) 12   (b) 6   (c) 7   (d) 8

19. Fill in the blanks.

A. Straight line	B. Unequal
C. 4	D. 8
E. 0	F. Equal
G. Cylinder	H. 12
I. 2	

1. All sides of a square are ______.

2. A cuboid has ______ edges.

3. There are ______ corners in a cylinder.

4. A pole is an example of a ______.

	1	2	3	4			1	2	3	4
(a)	C	D	I	A		(b)	B	H	D	G
(c)	F	H	E	G		(d)	F	D	I	A

20. State 'T' for true and 'F' for false.

1. A cuboid has 6 rectangular faces.

2.   consists of 3 cubes.

3.   is made up of only curved lines.

4. A sphere has more corners than a cone.

	1	2	3	4			1	2	3	4
(a)	F	T	F	T		(b)	F	T	T	T
(c)	T	T	T	F		(d)	T	F	T	F

Pattern

1. Complete the following pattern.

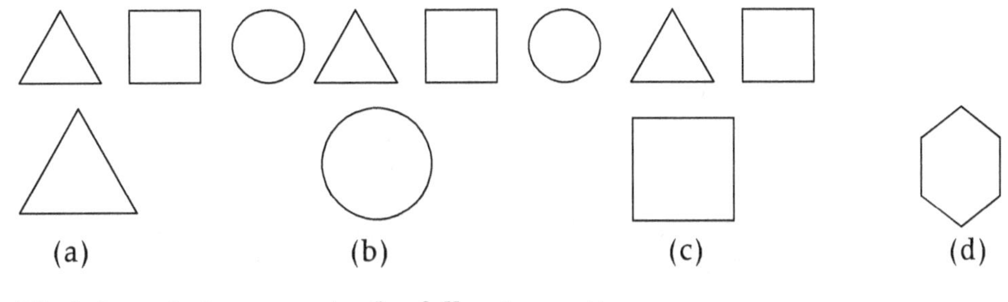

    (a)   (b)   (c)   (d)

2. Find the missing term in the following pattern.

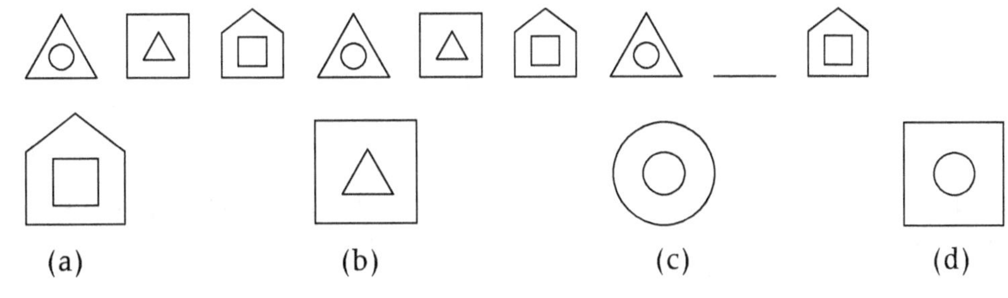

    (a)   (b)   (c)   (d)

3. Find the missing term in the following pattern.

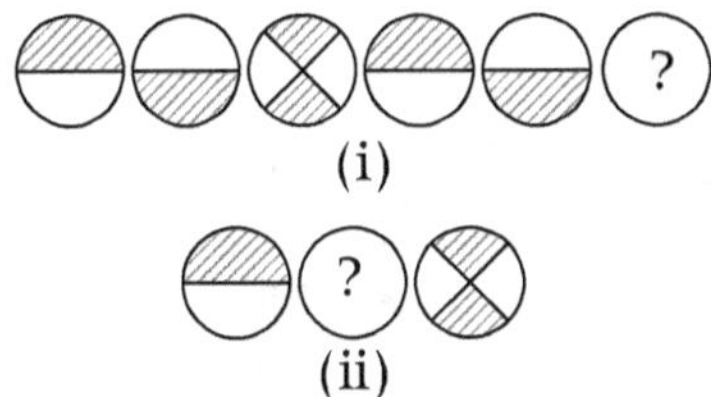

(i)

(ii)

(i)   (ii)   (i)   (ii)   (i)   (ii)   (i)   (ii)
   (a)   (b)   (c)   (d)

4. Mona is practising of dance. Her steps form a pattern. Identify the pattern and find her next step.

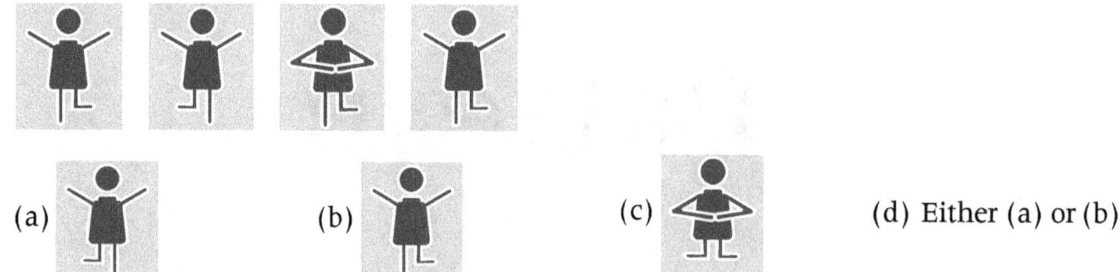

(a)   (b)   (c)   (d) Either (a) or (b)

5. What will be the colour of 21st bead, if the pattern continues?

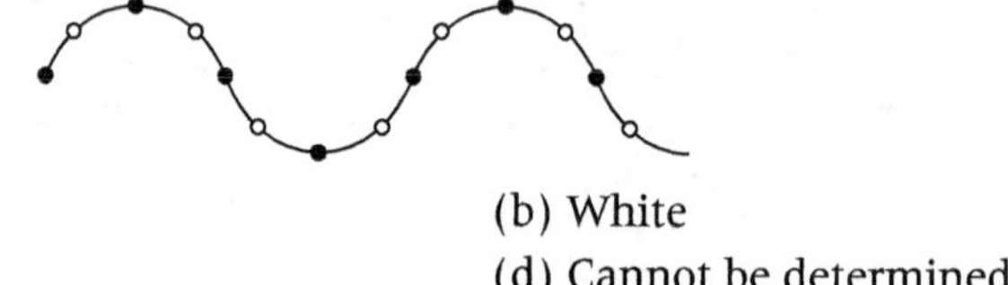

(a) Black   (b) White
(c) Neither (a) nor (b)   (d) Cannot be determined

6. A teacher shows four patterns to students. Three of them have similar repeating pattern. Look at the pattern and identify which one is different.

(a) || — || — || — ||—

(b) ✯ ✯ ✯ □ ✯ ✯ ✯ □ ✯ ✯ ✯ □

(c) × × + × × + × × +

(d) ○ ○ △ ○ ○ △ ○ ○ △

7. Observe the given pattern and if the pattern continue in the same way. Which of the following will be the 8th term?

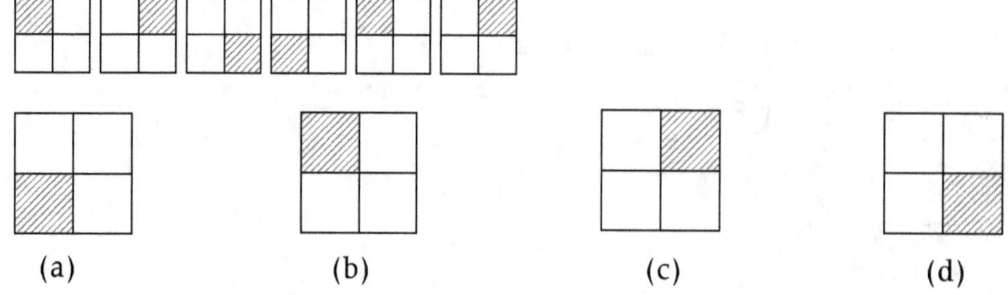

(a)   (b)   (c)   (d)

8. A key has a code which is used to open the lock which has the same code. Which figure shows the lock, which can be opened by the given key?

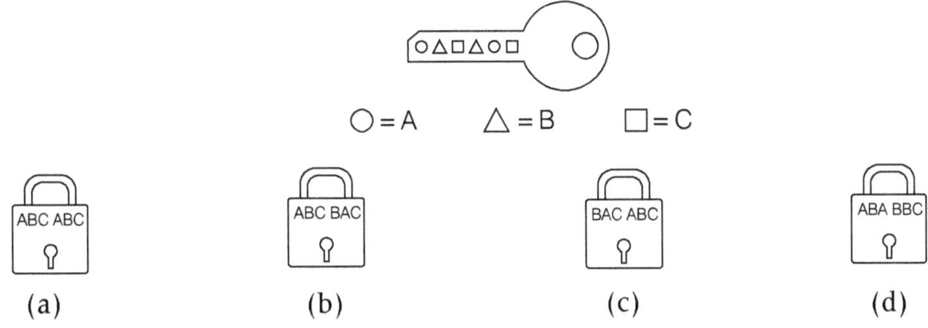

$\bigcirc = A \qquad \triangle = B \qquad \square = C$

(a)   (b)   (c)   (d)

9. Complete the following pattern.

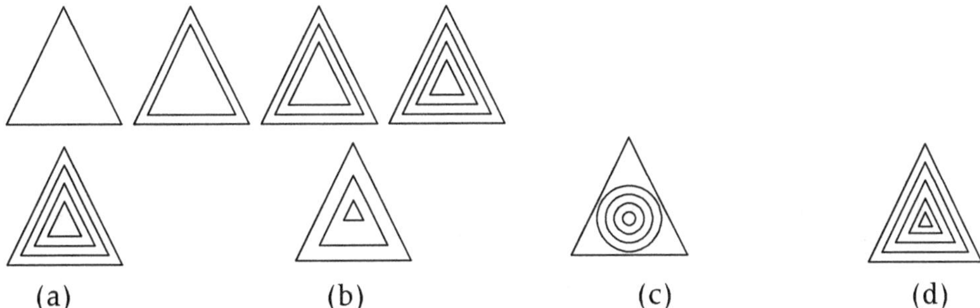

(a)   (b)   (c)   (d)

10. Complete the following pattern.

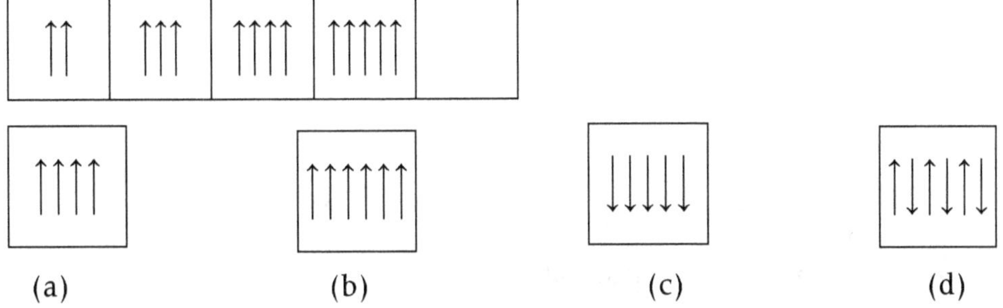

(a)   (b)   (c)   (d)

11. Identify the incorrect figure in the following pattern.

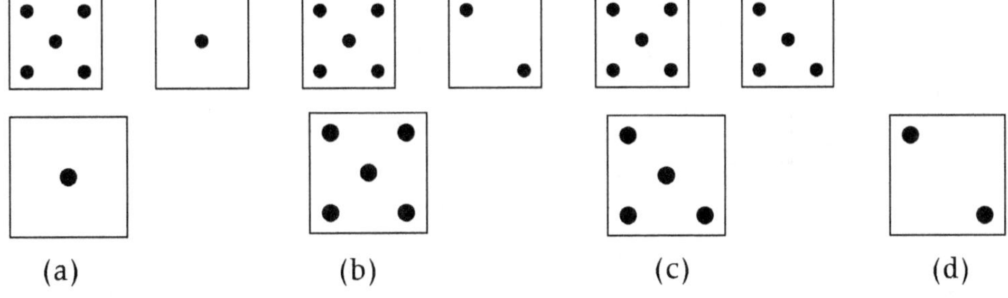

(a)   (b)   (c)   (d)

12. Find the next figure in the given pattern.

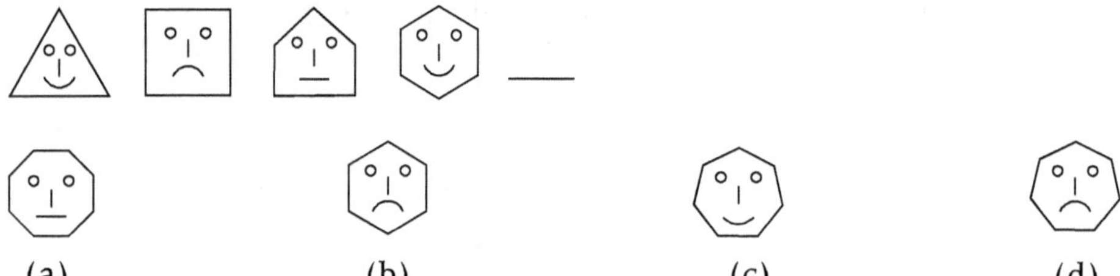

    (a)   (b)   (c)   (d)

13. Sayer has some wheels with an arrow mark. He arranged them in a pattern.

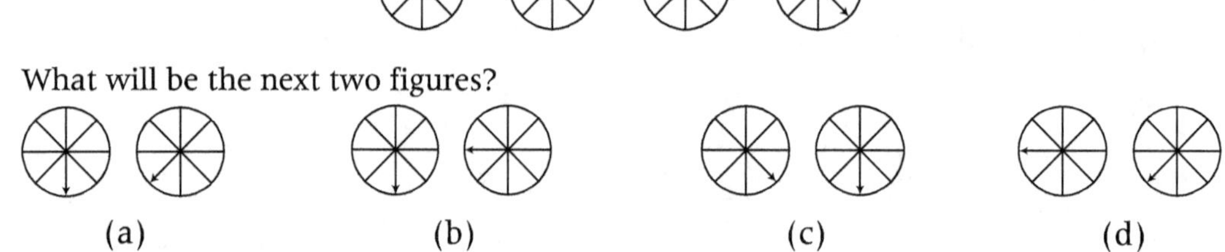

What will be the next two figures?

    (a)   (b)   (c)   (d)

14. Complete the pattern by selecting the correct figure from the given options.

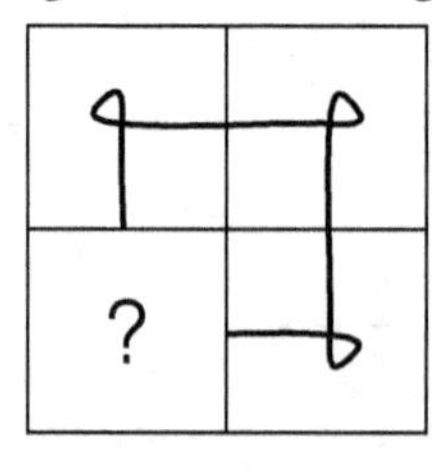

    (a)   (b)   (c)   (d)

15. Complete the pattern by choosing suitable option.

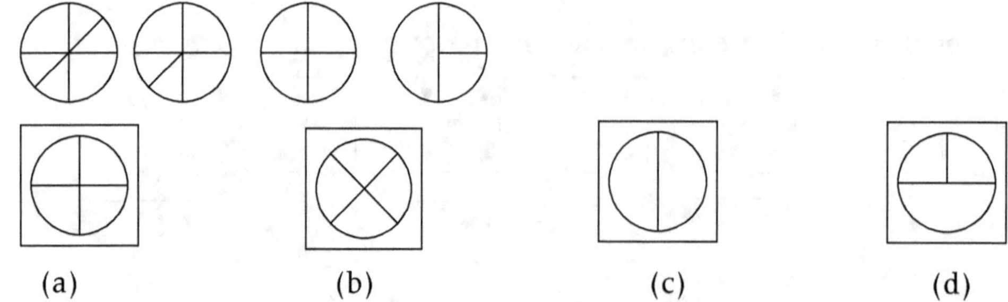

    (a)   (b)   (c)   (d)

16. What will be the missing term in the following pattern?

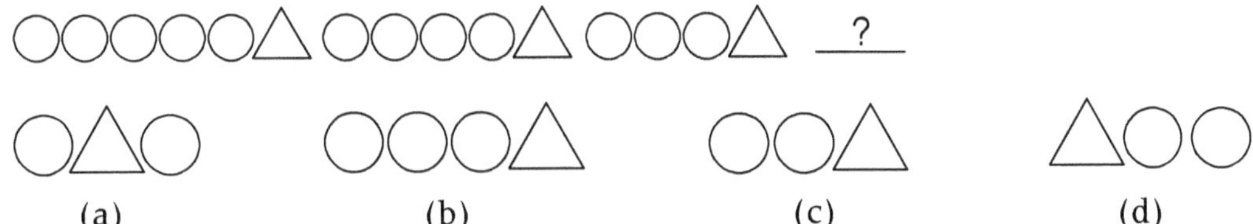

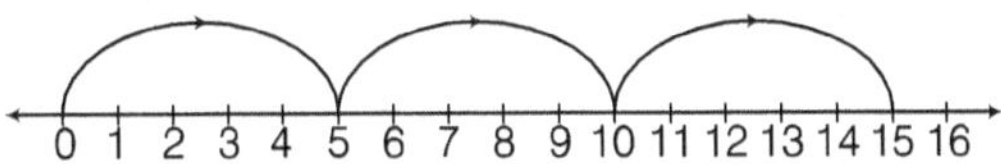

(a)   (b)   (c)   (d)

17. The following number line represents a pattern. Identify the pattern and choose the correct option.

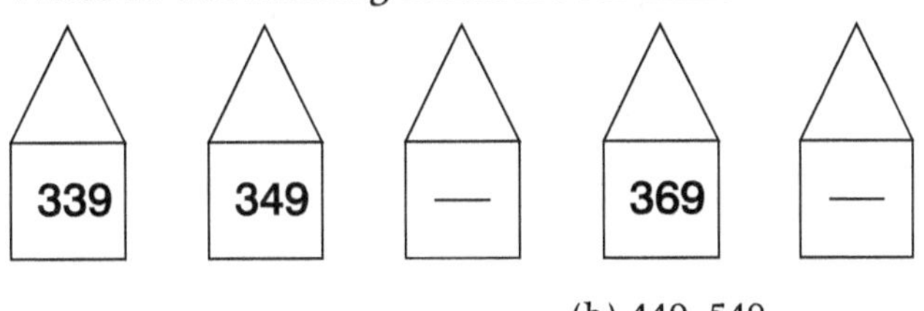

(a) Skip counting by 2   (b) Skip counting by 5
(c) Skip counting by 3   (d) None of these

18. Mr. Jones delivers letters on central street. He finds some of the house numbers are difficult to see. Write in the missing numbers for him.

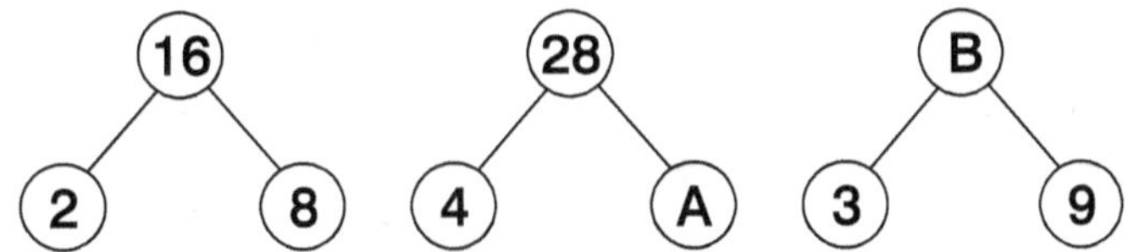

(a) 379, 389   (b) 449, 549
(c) 359, 379   (d) 349, 449

19. Kate draw the following pattern on the board.

$$1I\ 2S\ 3E\ 4P\ 5\partial\ \_\_$$

Find the next term in the above pattern.

7ᒇ   6ə   9P   88
(a)   (b)   (c)   (d)

Directions (Q. Nos. 20 and 21) Study the following pattern.

16 — 2, 8   28 — 4, A   B — 3, 9

20. The missing number A is ...
(a) 6   (b) 7   (c) 8   (d) 9

21. The sum of A and B is ...
(a) 27   (b) 35   (c) 33   (d) 34

Data Handling

1. Lisa drew the following shapes in her maths notebook.

Using the above shapes, fill the given table.

Name	Number of figures drawn
Triangle	A
Circle	B
Rectangle	C
Square	D

	A	B	C	D
(a)	5	5	3	2
(b)	3	2	5	4
(c)	4	5	3	3
(d)	5	5	2	3

Directions (Q. Nos. 2 and 3) Some children were playing a game. They collected cards with ladybirds on them. Here are the cards they had at the end of the game. Study the information and answer the questions.

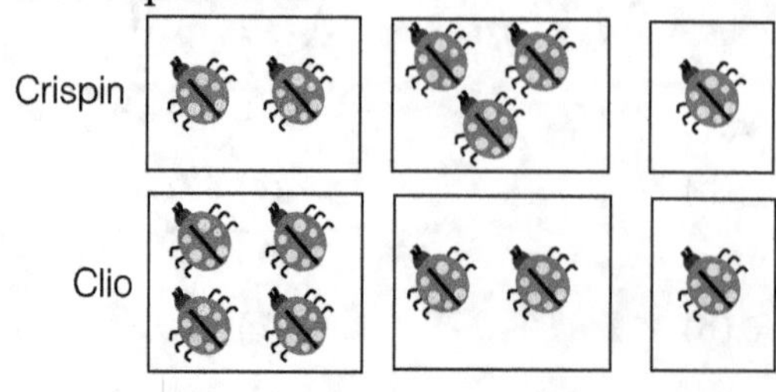

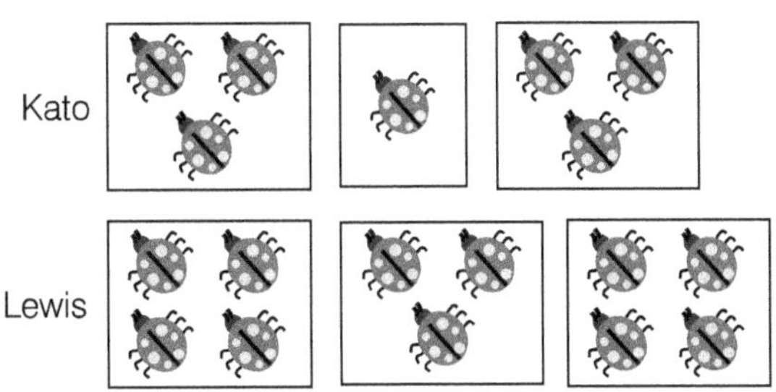

2. Which child wins the game by collecting the most ladybirds?

   (a) Crispin   (b) Clio   (c) Kato   (d) Lewis

3. Which child loses the game by collecting the lowest ladybirds?

   (a) Crispin   (b) Clio   (c) Kato   (d) Lewis

4. A shopkeeper has many types of board games such as chess, drafts etc. He asked his customer to vote for their favourite board game. Graph given below shows the votes of 15 children.

   Study the above information and find out how many children likes monopoly.

   (a) 2   (b) 6   (c) 4   (d) 5

5. Uncle Philo has a bakery shop. The picture given below shows the number of cakes sold in his bakery. Use the picture and answer the following questions.

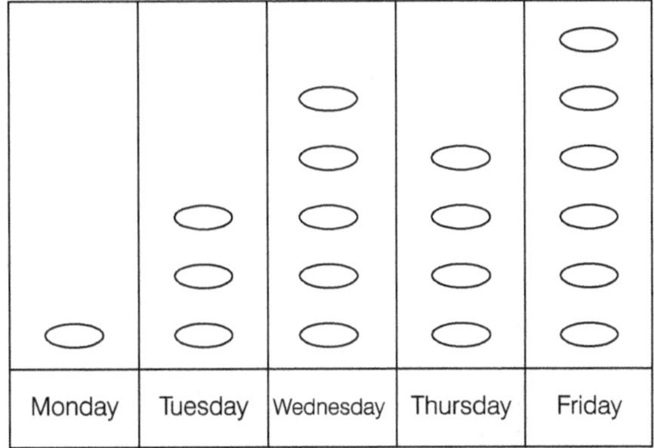

Each ⬭ = 2 cake
How many cakes did uncle Philo sell in this week?

(a) 20   (b) 40   (c) 19   (d) 38

Directions (Q. Nos. 6 and 7) Bhavya asked some shoppers how they had travelled to supermarket, then he drew a pictogram to show his results.

Car	👤 👤 👤 👤 👤
Bus	👤 👤 👤 👤 👤 👤
Walk	👤 👤
Bicycle	👤 👤 👤 👤

Each 👤 = 2 person

6. How many less people travelled by car than bus?

(a) 3   (b) 2   (c) 4   (d) 6

7. If Bhavya surveyed 40 shoppers, then how many shoppers used other than the given transport?

(a) 8   (b) 10   (c) 7   (d) 6

Directions (Q. Nos. 8 and 9) Daniel, a farmer has some farm animals. Picture graph below shows the number of animals in his farm. Use this picture graph to answer the questions.

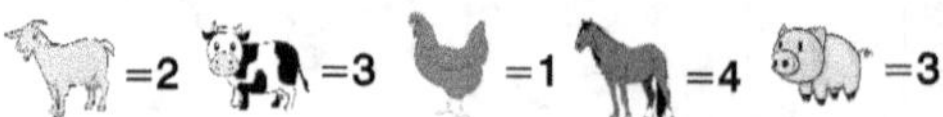

8. Which animal is fewest?

(a) Cow   (b) Chicken   (c) Horse   (d) Pig

9. What is the total number of animals in Daniel's farm?

(a) 32   (b) 34   (c) 30   (d) 28

Directions (Q. Nos. 10 and 11) The following table shows the number of trees planted by some students in July. Study the graph and answer the questions.

Theon	🌳 🌳 🌳 🌳 🌳
Cody	🌳 🌳 🌳 🌳 🌳
John	🌳 🌳 🌳 🌳
Jonas	🌳 🌳 🌳 🌳 🌳
Cyrus	🌳 🌳 🌳 🌳 🌳 🌳 🌳

10. If the target of students was to plant a total of 30 trees, then how many more trees they need to plant?

    (a) 2   (b) 3   (c) 4   (d) 5

11. Use the above information to find out the correct statement.
    (a) Cyrus planted maximum trees
    (b) Theon and Jonas planted the same number of trees
    (c) John planted the least number of trees
    (d) All are correct

12. Philo, Cosmo, Marcus and Nero collected some picture cards.

Philo	🏏 🏏 🏏 🏏 🏏 🏏
Cosmo	🏏 🏏 🏏 🏏 🏏
Marcus	🏏 🏏 🏏 🏏 🏏 🏏 🏏
Nero	🏏 🏏 🏏 🏏

Each 🏏 = 50 cards

Match the following children with the correct number of cards.

1. Philo	A. 250
2. Cosmo	B. 200
3. Marcus	C. 300
4. Nero	D. 350

	1	2	3	4		1	2	3	4		1	2	3	4		1	2	3	4
(a)	D	A	C	B	(b)	C	D	A	B	(c)	B	C	D	A	(d)	C	A	D	B

13. A student lives in a village. He recorded the electricity bills of 10 houses in that village as given below:

House Number	Electricity bill
1	324
2	700
3	617
4	400
5	356
6	365
7	435
8	548
9	736
10	780

Which house has maximum electricity bill among 10 houses?
(a) 2nd　　　　　(b) 9th　　　　　(c) 3rd　　　　　(d) 10th

14. The heights of four friends are given in the following table:

Anna	100 centimetres
Kate	98 centimetres
Suzanne	108 centimetres
Peri	112 centimetres

All the girls stands in a queue (in decreasing order of height) as shown below :

Identify the position of Suzanne.
(a) 1st　　　　　(b) 2nd　　　　　(c) 3rd　　　　　(d) 4th

Directions (Q. Nos. 15 and 16) Stoffel planted a tree five months back. The height of the tree in each month is given below:

March	20 centimetres
April	50 centimetres
May	100 centimetres
June	120 centimetres
July	160 centimetres

15. In which month did the height of the tree increases the most?

(a) April   (b) May   (c) June   (d) July

16. What is the overall increases in the height of tree from March till July?

(a) 2 metres   (b) 140 centimetres

(c) 40 centimetres   (d) 160 centimetres

Directions (Q. Nos. 17 and 18) The given table gives the information about the number of subjects engaged in different activities:

Activity	Number of students
Cycling	36
Running	19
Swimming	23
Music	6

Now, answer the following questions.

17. In which Activity the maximum and minimum number of students engaged?

	Maximum	Minimum
(a)	Running	Music
(b)	Cycling	Swimming
(c)	Music	Running
(d)	Cycling	Music

18. Number of students engaged in cycling and swimming together?

(a) 95   (b) 59   (c) 42   (d) 55

Directions (Q. Nos. 19 and 20) Lisa noted sunrise and sunset time on four days. Use this information to answer the given questions.

Date	Sunrise	Sunset
1st July	5 : 00 am	6 : 30 pm
2nd July	5 : 30 am	7 : 00 pm
3rd July	6 : 00 am	6 : 30 pm
4th July	5 : 30 am	6 : 00 pm

19. What was the time difference between sunset and sunrise on 4th July?

(a) 12 hours 30 minutes   (b) 13 hours

(c) 12 hours   (d) 13 hours 30 minutes

20. How many minutes earlier is the sunset on 4th July than on 2nd July?

(a) 30 minutes   (b) 45 minutes

(c) 60 minutes   (d) 120 minutes

PRACTICE SET  01

1. Convert ₹ 500 into paise.
(a) 50000 paise   (b) 5000 paise
(c) 500 paise   (d) 50 paise

2. What come next in place of question mark?

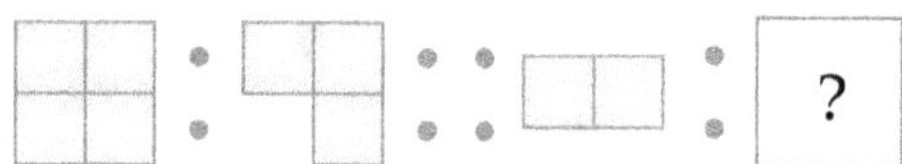

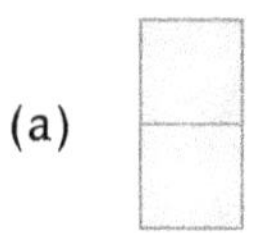 (a)   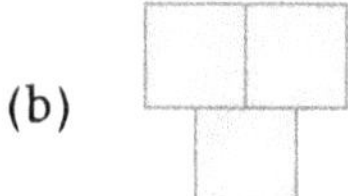 (b)

 (c)    (d)

3. Five dices were showing 3 dots each on its upper side on rolling. What is the total number of dots five dices will have?

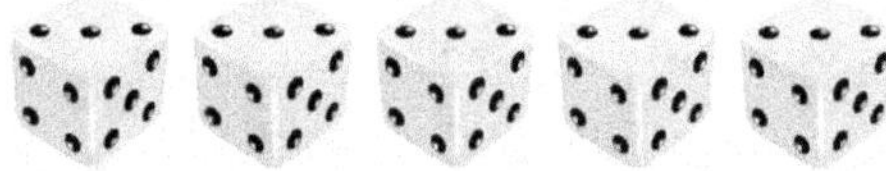

(a) 20   (b) 22   (c) 15   (d) 24

4. What time does the clock show in the figure below?

(a) 10 : 05   (b) 10 : 50
(c) 10 : 10   (d) 10 : 40

5. If dividend is 72 and divisor is 5, then what will be remainder (R) and quotient (Q)?
(a) $R = 1, Q = 5$ (b) $R = 5, Q = 14$
(c) $R = 2, Q = 14$ (d) None of these

6. Write the largest 3 digit number formed by using the following digit.
4, 9, 6
(a) 964   (b) 946   (c) 649   (d) 469

7. The figure given below is formed by 2 curves and .... straight lines.

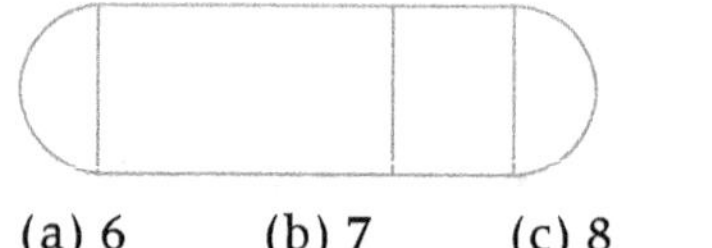

(a) 6   (b) 7   (c) 8   (d) 5

8. Match the objects in List-I with the standard unit used for their measurement in List-II.

	List-I		List-II
A.		1.	Metre
B.		2.	Kilogram
C.		3.	Litre
D.		4.	Centimetre

Codes

	A	B	C	D		A	B	C	D
(a)	2	1	4	2	(b)	4	2	1	3
(c)	1	3	4	2	(d)	3	4	2	1

9. Find the addition of the numbers given inside the triangle.

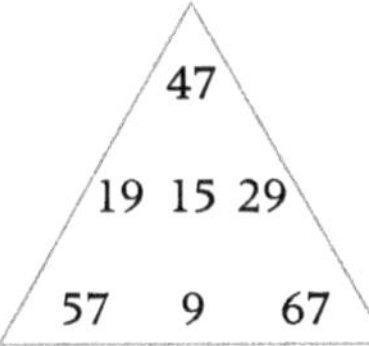

        47
    19 15 29
   57   9   67

(a) 243   (b) 263   (c) 250   (d) 259

10. Read the following data carefully and answer the given question.

Classes	Number of Students
Class 3	30
Class 4	35
Class 5	30
Class 6	28
Class 7	48

What is the total number of students in all classes?

(a) 161   (b) 171   (c) 165   (d) 175

11. What is the expanded form of the given number.

249

(a) $200 + 4 + 9$ (b) $200 + 40 + 9$
(c) $400 + 2 + 90$ (d) $20 + 40 + 9$

12. What will be the next term in the given pattern?

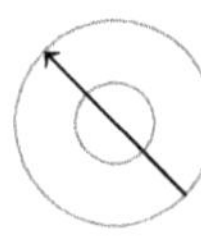
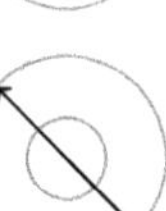
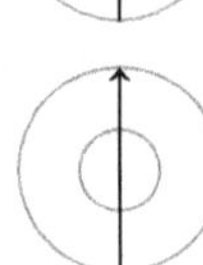

(a) 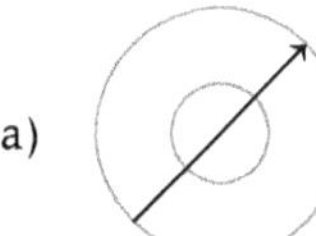   (b) 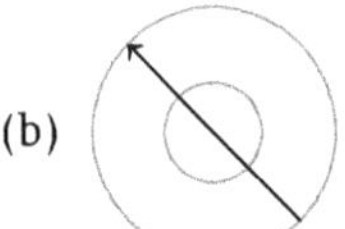

(c) 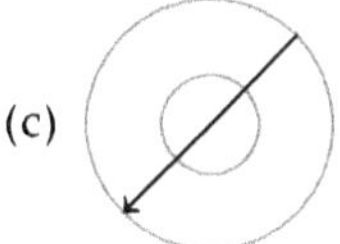   (d) 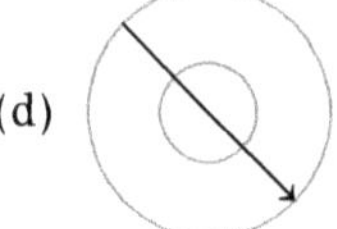

13. Look at the image carefully. How many total beads are there in necklaces? Each necklace is made up of 10 beads.

(a) 30   (b) 48
(c) 50   (d) 42

14. How many triangles are there in the given figure?

(a) 4   (b) 6
(c) 5   (d) 7

15. Soumya has 3 boxes. Each box has 6 sweets in it. She gave 5 sweets to his brother. How many sweets are left with Soumya?

(a) 12
(b) 16
(c) 18
(d) 13

16. Add the value of given money.

(a) ₹ 180   (b) ₹ 178
(c) ₹ 181   (d) ₹ 175

17. A small tin contains 2 L of paint. A large tin contains 4 times as much as small tin. Aleena bought the given tin of paint. How much paint did she buy altogether?

(a) 36 L   (b) 48 L
(c) 32 L   (d) 40 L

18. A book has 98 pages. Divya has read 69 pages out of them. How many more pages does she has to read to finish the book?

(a) 30   (b) 28
(c) 29   (d) 32

19. Add the following:
5 h 11 min, 4 h 30 min, 7 h 10 min

(a) 16 h 51 min   (b) 15 h 51 min
(c) 16 h 45 min   (d) None of these

20. Kate need some coloured paper to complete her school project. She bought 12 green coloured papers, 15 blue coloured paper, 9 yellow coloured paper and 18 red coloured papers.

If  = 3 papers, then which of the following pictograph is correct?

(a)

Green	
Blue	
Yellow	
Red	

(b)

Green	
Blue	
Yellow	
Red	

(c)

Green	
Blue	
Yellow	
Red	

(d) None of the above

21. Choose the correct option to complete the pattern.

75 95 115 135 ?

(a) 145   (b) 155
(c) 165   (d) 175

22. What would be the total cost of 2 kg of potato at the rate of ₹ 25 per kg and 4 kg of brinjal at the rate of ₹ 20 per kg?

(a) ₹ 135   (b) ₹ 125
(c) ₹ 120   (d) ₹ 130

23. The chessboard consists of squares arranged in two alternating colours (white and black). How many black squares are present in chess board?

(a) 28　　　　　　　(b) 32
(c) 30　　　　　　　(d) 34

24. There are 3680 sheets of paper. If 16 bundles are to be made with equal number of sheets, how many sheets will be there in each bundle?
(a) 250　　　　　　　(b) 230
(c) 240　　　　　　　(d) None of these

25. Palak bought a dress for ₹ 268 and a bag for ₹ 195. How much money the shopkeeper returned, if Palak gave him a note of ₹ 500?
(a) ₹ 37　　　　　　　(b) ₹ 35
(c) ₹ 40　　　　　　　(d) ₹ 30

26. State 'T' for true and 'F' for false for the given statements.
　I. $\boxed{634}$ has $\boxed{34}$ tens.
　II. Adding 19 to 23 will give an even number.
　III. 5 figures has 10 eyes.
```
    I    II   III
(a) F    F    T
(b) T    T    T
(c) F    T    T
(d) T    F    T
```

27. Choose the incorrect one.
(a) $550 + 78 > 425 + 169$
(b) $339 - 89 < 435 - 150$
(c) $189 + 407 = 483 + 113$
(d) $215 + 59 > 165 + 145$

28. There are 52 students in class 5 section A, 45 in section B. How many total students are there in section A and B?
(a) 100　　　　　　　(b) 90
(c) 95　　　　　　　(d) 97

29. If today is June 30, what will be the date on the day after tomorrow?
(a) September 2　　　(b) July 2
(c) July 1　　　　　　(d) None of these

30. Find the missing number, if some rule is followed in all the three figures.

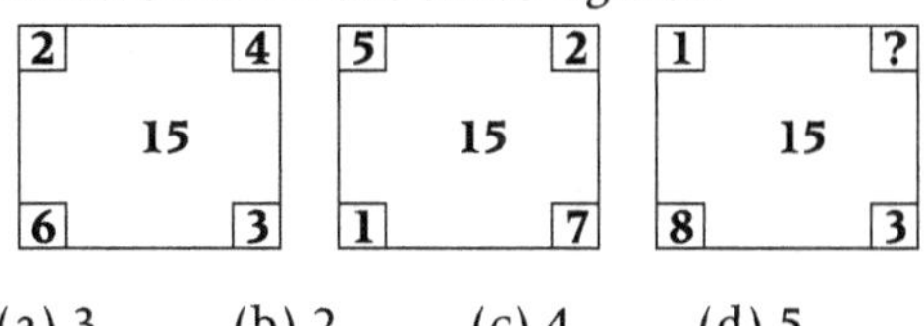

(a) 3　　　(b) 2　　　(c) 4　　　(d) 5

31. Priya formed a 3-digit number using the given cards

$\boxed{1}\ \boxed{3}\ \boxed{5}\ \boxed{7}$

The digit at ones place is 6 more than the digit at ten's place. The digit at hundreds place is 4 more than the digit at tens place. What is the number?
(a) 137　(b) 517　(c) 513　(d) 715

32. Consider the following diagram:

| A | 250 grams | B | | A | 40 grams |

| C | 30 grams | | 300 grams |

Which of the box is heaviest?

(a) A

(b) B

(c) C

(d) None of the above

33. Suraj starts his cricket practice on 14th October 20XX. He practices for 3 days and then he takes a break for 5 days. He again practice for 1 week. His practice finishes on ....

October 20XX						
Sun	Mon	Tue	Wed	Thu	Fri	Sat
1	2	3	4	5	6	7
8	9	10	11	12	13	14
15	16	17	18	19	20	21
22	23	24	25	26	27	28
29	30	31				

(a) 27th October

(b) 28th October

(c) 29th October

(d) 23rd October

Directions (Q. Nos. 34 and 35) A bookshop sells different varieties of books. The given graph shows how many of each they sold in August.

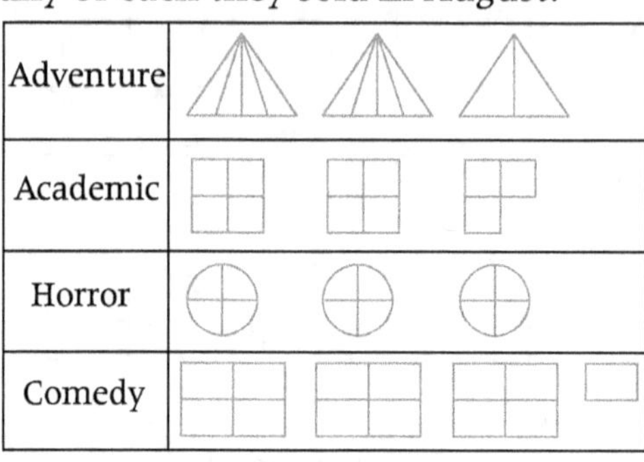

34. The shop had 20 adventure books in the beginning of August. How many of these books have left at the end of August?

(a) 20   (b) 15   (c) 10   (d) 12

35. How many books did the shop sell altogether?

(a) 44   (b) 46   (c) 56   (d) 42

PRACTICE SET 02

1. 17 tens – 7 ones = ... tens ... ones.
   (a) 16, 3   (b) 1, 63   (c) 13, 6   (d) 6, 13

2. A postman delivered 132 letters on Monday and 269 letters on Tuesday. How many letters did he deliver altogether?
   (a) 391
   (b) 491
   (c) 401
   (d) 301

3. When Jerry planted a tree it was 12 centimetres tall. Now, the plant is 26 centimetres tall. Which of the following scale correctly shows the increase in height of the tree?

(a) 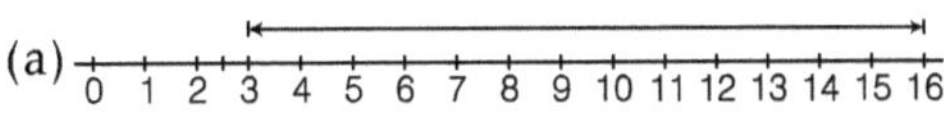

(b) 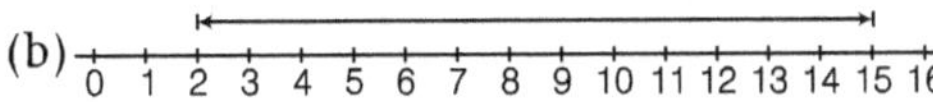

(c) 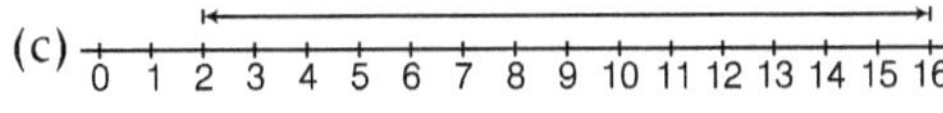

(d) 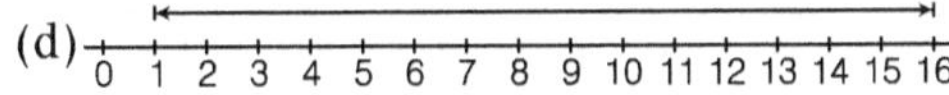

4. Find the missing number z.

$$
\begin{array}{r}
6\ \ 8\ \ 9 \\
-1\ \ 3\ \ z \\
\hline
z\ \ 5\ \ 4 \\
\hline
\end{array}
$$

   (a) 3
   (c) 5
   (b) 4
   (d) 6

5. Carol was born on 18th October. Kimi was born on Gandhi Jayanti. Who is older and by how many days?
   (a) Carol, 16 days
   (b) Kimi, 16 days
   (c) Carol, 18 days
   (d) Kimi, 14 days

6. Given,

Following the pattern, identify the total number of dots in E and F.
   (a) 14   (b) 13   (c) 12   (d) 11

7. Which of the following figures is made up of six straight lines and three curved lines?

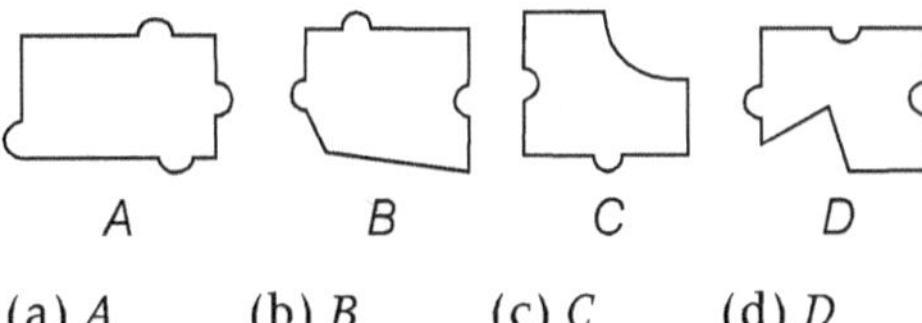

   (a) A   (b) B   (c) C   (d) D

8. Daniel has three times as much as Sani. Sani has ₹ 8. Kary has ₹ 25 more than Daniel. How much money does Kary have?
   (a) ₹ 24   (b) ₹ 33   (c) ₹ 40   (d) ₹ 49

9. Study the given pattern and find the missing number.

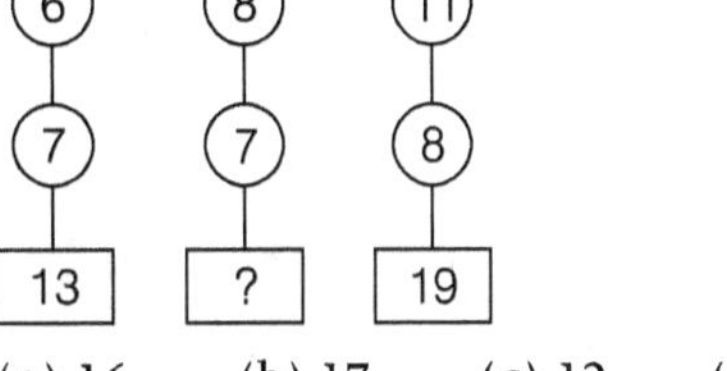

   (a) 16   (b) 17   (c) 12   (d) 15

10. Nick's class is playing a game. Each student has a bag with different cards. The given table shows the points of each card

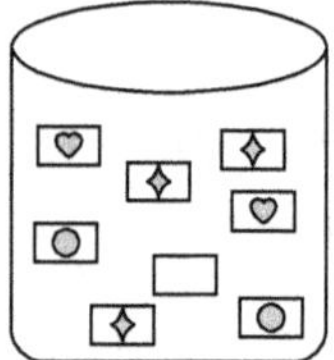

1	♡	2 points
1	◇	10 points
1	●	20 points

This is Nick's bag

How many points does Nick have?

(a) 74   (b) 70   (c) 32   (d) 63

Directions (Q. Nos. 11-12) Study the following figures and answer the questions that follow.

11. How many glasses of water does it need to fill the bucket completely?

(a) 9   (b) 6   (c) 5   (d) 8

12. If ▯ = 2 litres, then how much amount of water does a tank hold?

(a) 30 litres   (b) 6 litres
(c) 18 litres   (d) 36 litres

13. Study following table

	Even number	Odd number
Less than 100	A	B
Greater than 100	C	D

Which number should go in B?

(a) 101   (b) 100   (c) 99   (d) 98

14. I am a 2-digit number. I am more than 10 but less than 15. I occur in the multiplication tables of both 2 and 3. What number am I?

(a) 11   (b) 12   (c) 13   (d) 14

15. Which letter contains the most number of curved lines?

(a) A   (b) B   (c) C   (d) D

16. Carol skipped 10 times on the first day, 12 times on 2nd day, 14 times on 3rd day and so on. How many times did he skip altogether for 6 days?

(a) 110   (b) 80   (c) 100   (d) 90

17. The given clock shows the time at which Zenith went to school everyday.

It takes her 30 minutes to reach the school and there is a zero period of 1 hour 30 minutes.

At what time the zero period gets over?

(a) 10 : 00 am   (b) 10 : 00 pm
(c) 10 : 30 am   (d) 10 : 30 pm

18. What comes next in the pattern given below?

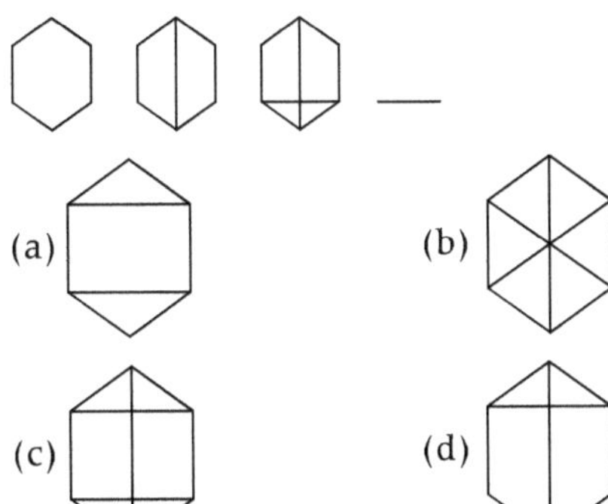

(a)   (b)

(c)   (d)

19. Garnet has two containers filled with water. She wants to fill the container *B* upto 550 litres with water from container *A*. How much water will be left in container *A*?

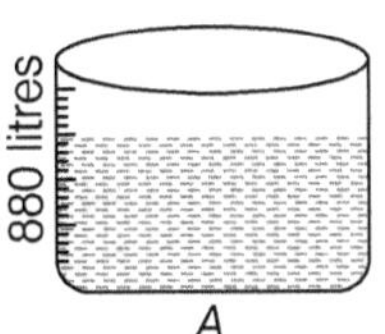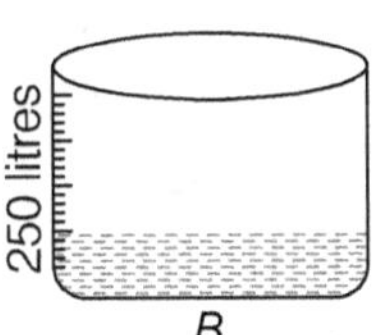

(a) 680 litres   (b) 300 litres
(c) 580 litres   (d) 800 litres

20. The distance between each lamppost is given below. If lampposts are at equal distance, then how far will the first lamppost from the fifth lamppost?

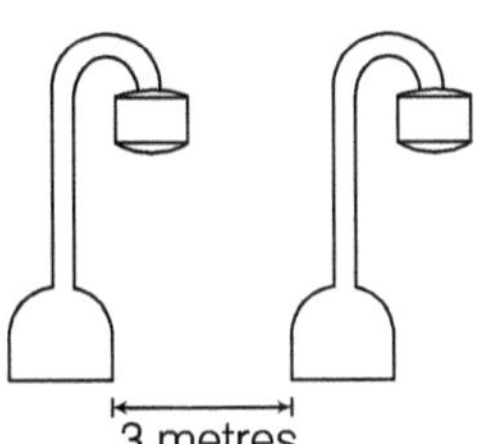

(a) 8 metres   (b) 15 metres
(c) 9 metres   (d) 12 metres

21. The parking charges of a showroom are as follow

Time	Charges per hour
9:00 am-10:00 am	₹ 2
10:00 am-12:00 pm	₹ 4
12:00 pm-4:00 pm	₹ 6
4:00 pm-8:00 pm	₹ 8

If Cyra parked her car from 10:00 am to 4:00 pm, then how much amount did she pay?
(a) ₹ 30   (b) ₹ 32
(c) ₹ 10   (d) ₹ 18

22. Each of the shape has the following value

$\triangle = 7$, $\square = 17$

In which of the following option the value of circle is different, if the value of the shapes are being added together?

(a) $\triangle \ \square \ \bigcirc$ = 30

(b) $\triangle \ \square \triangle \bigcirc$ = 37

(c) $\triangle \square \ \square \bigcirc$ = 47

(d) $\triangle \ \triangle \bigcirc \square \triangle \bigcirc$ = 100

23. The price of a book is ₹ 24 and a pencil box is ₹ 54. If there is sale of half-price in a shop. How much money is needed to purchase a book and a pencil box?
(a) ₹ 39   (b) ₹ 30
(c) ₹ 20   (d) ₹ 78

24. Manju wants to share 30 toffees with her 5 friends. How many toffees will each of her friend get?
(a) 7   (b) 6
(c) 9   (d) 4

25. How many squares are present in the given figure?

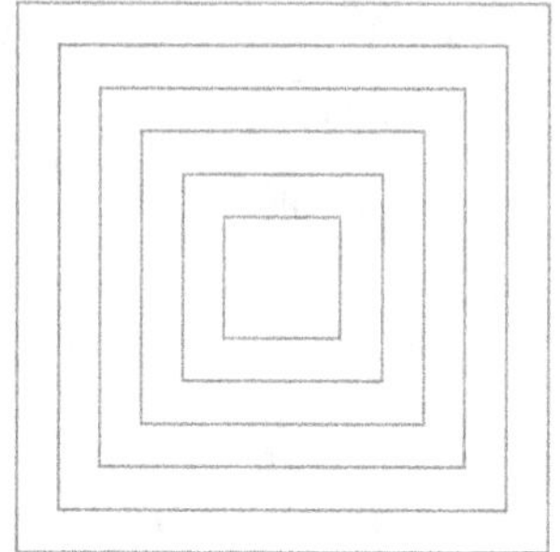

(a) 7   (b) 5   (c) 8   (d) 6

26. How much money you need to buy the following articles?

Lays—₹ 20; Glucon-D—₹ 89

Bread—₹ 40; Cold drink—₹ 75

(a) ₹ 224   (b) ₹ 225

(c) ₹ 223   (d) ₹ 200

27. Jitesh has to take 18 steps of a stair case to go to first floor. How many steps Jitesh has to take while going up and down once?

(a) 28   (b) 30   (c) 36   (d) 34

28. Which is the longest tooth brush?

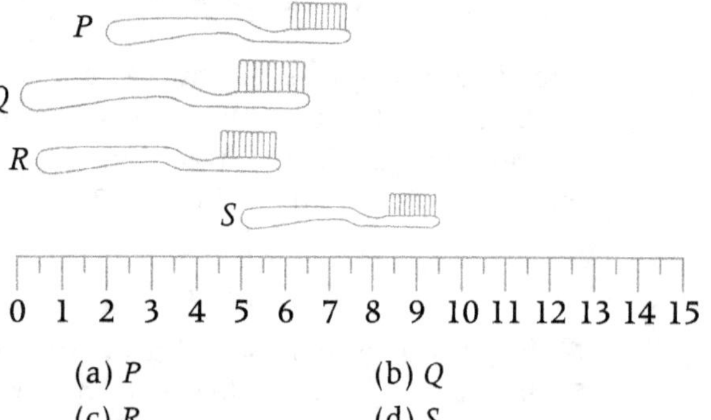

(a) P   (b) Q

(c) R   (d) S

29. How many numbers given in the following figure are exactly divisible by 2?

(a) 4   (b) 5

(c) 6   (d) 11

30. Match the following columns.

Column I	Column II
P. 15×3	1. 30
Q. $4 + 4 + 4$	2. 6×4
R. 6 groups of 5	3. 3×4
S. $8 + 8 + 8$	4. 45

	P	Q	R	S		P	Q	R	S
(a)	2	3	1	4	(b)	4	1	3	2
(c)	2	1	4	3	(d)	4	3	1	2

31. Each side of pentagon is 5m long, then what is the length of rope needed to form the pentagon?

(a) 25 m   (b) 30 m

(c) 20 m   (d) 40 m

32. In the given figure how many horizontal lines are present.

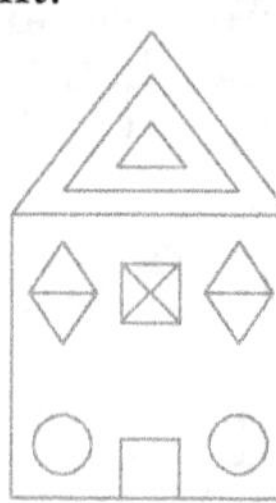

(a) 9   (b) 7

(c) 10   (d) 8

Directions (Q. Nos. 33 and 34) The table gives the number of tickets sold for different rides in 'SPLASH' theme park on Saturday.

Riders	Tickets Sold
My fair lady	
Giant wheel	
Horse ride	
Roller coaster	
Water ride	
Topsy turyy	
Each = 10 and = 5	

33. How many tickets were sold for the Roller coaster?

(a) 60   (b) 45
(c) 55   (d) 40

34. How many tickets were sold for My Fair Lady and water Ride altogether?

(a) 60   (b) 55
(c) 80   (d) 65

35. Akshita bought the toys shown below:

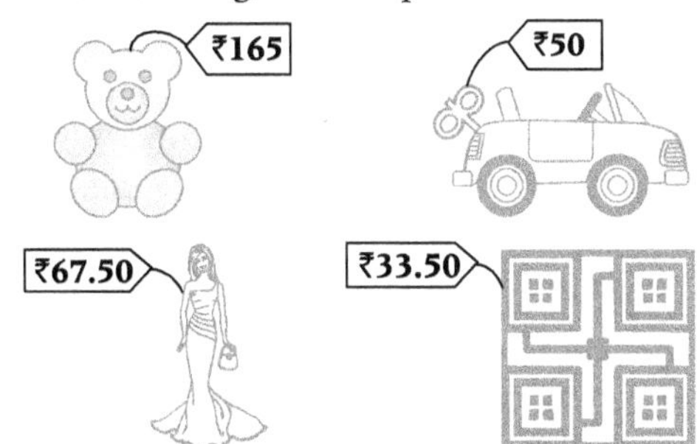

Match the toys (List I) with the enough money (List II) that is needed to purchase them

List-I (Toys)	**List-II** (Enough Money)
A. Toy car	1. ₹ 70
B. Barbie doll	2. ₹ 175
C. Ludo	3. ₹ 60
D. Teddy	4. ₹ 35

Codes

	A	B	C	D		A	B	C	D
(a)	3	1	4	2	(b)	3	2	1	4
(c)	4	3	1	2	(d)	2	1	4	3

Hints & Solutions

1. Odd Numbers

1. *(d)* As we know the numbers that have 1, 3, 5, 7 and 9 in, its ones place, are called odd number.

Clearly, we can see, cost of balloon in Rohit's hand is ₹ 19 and 19 is a odd number.

2. *(c)* The correct sequence of decreasing order of given number is $397 > 379 > 378 > 371$

Hence, option (c) is required answer.

3. *(b)* As we know,

Out of 193, 70, 35 and 15, only 70 have 0 in its ones place.

Thus, 70 is an even number.

So, the life span of elephant is an even number.

4. *(c)* Out of ₹ 21, ₹ 23, ₹ 25 and ₹ 26, only 26 have 6 in its ones place.

Thus, ₹ 26 is an even number.

Hence, option (c) is correct.

5. *(b)* Interchanging the 1st and 3rd digits of 942, we get

$$9 \quad 4 \quad 2 = 249$$

So, the cost of the olympaid book is ₹ 249.

6. *(a)* $67 = 60 + 7 = 6 \times 10 + 7 \times 1 = 6$ tens $+ 7$ ones

So, the place value of 7 is ones.

7. *(d)* We know that, largest 3-digit number $= 999$

So, the place value of 9 in 999 is hundreds, tens and ones.

8. *(d)* As per given options,

Option (a) If we place two beads at tens place, then the number will be 322.

Option (b) If we place three beads at tens place, then the number will be 332.

Option (c) If we place one bead at tens place, then the number will be 312.

Option (d) If we place no beads at tens place, then the number will be 302, which is smallest among others.

Hence, option (d) is correct.

9. *(b)* Given that the number of carrots planted is more than 420

Among the given options, each number is more than 420, but only 389 is less than 420.

So, 389 cannot be the number of carrots planted by the old man.

10. *(d)* Considering option (d)

Clue 1 The number at tens place is double the number at ones place.

In the number 821, the number at ones place is 1 and the number at tens place is 2, which is double of 1.

So, Nikhil's puppy is given in option (d).

Which is more than one hundred sixty five and less than two hundred.

Hence, option (d) is correct.

11. *(a)* One hundred and seventy

Book blue fairy represent 170 pages.

$$= 170 = 100 + 70 = 100 + 70 + 0$$

So, Maria is reading Blue fairy.

12. *(c)* Two hundred and six $= 200 + 6 = 206$

From the given figure, it is clear that Fluffy ate 206 carrots. Which is more than two hundreds and 6 pm its ten's place.

13. *(c)* Number of pencils with Anand stationers

$$= 15 \text{ tens} + 3 \text{ ones}$$
$$= 15 \times 10 + 3 \times 1 = 150 + 3 = 153$$

Number of pencils with Curiosity stationers

$$= 2 \text{ hundreds} + 11 \text{ tens} + 5 \text{ ones}$$
$$= 2 \times 100 + 11 \times 10 + 5 \times 1$$
$$= 200 + 110 + 5 = 315$$

Number of pencils with JK stationers

$$= 51 \text{ tens} + 3 \text{ ones} + 0 \text{ ones}$$
$$= 51 \times 10 + 3 \times 1 + 0 \times 1$$
$$= 510 + 3 + 0 = 513$$

Number of pencils with Array's stationers

$$= 3 \text{ hundreds} + 51 \text{ ones}$$
$$= 3 \times 100 + 51 \times 1 = 300 + 51 = 351$$

So, statement given in option (c) is correct.

14. *(a)* Option (a) → Sixty nine can also be written as 69.

Option (b) → 7 more than $61 = 61 + 7 = 68$

Option (c) → 5 less than $67 = 67 - 5 = 62$

Option (d) → we know even number after sixty five (65) is 66.

So, option (a) i.e., 69 is largest among other options.

15. *(d)* Considering option (d),

$627 > 9 + 661 = 670$

We know that 670 is greater than 627.

so, option (d) is incorrect.

16. *(d)* Option (b) → Arranging the number of newspapers sold on different days in ascending order, we get

$$452 < 482 < 497 < 623 < 625$$

So, the number of newspapers sold on Thursday is highest.

So, option (b) is correct.

Option (c) → From the above arrangement, it is clear that the number of newspapers sold on Friday is smallest.

So, option (c) is correct.

Hence, the statements given in options (b) and (c) are correct.

17. *(a)* A. 2 tens 3 ones $= 2 \times 10 + 3 \times 1 = 20 + 3 = 23$

and 53 ones $= 53 \times 1 = 53$

Since, $23 < 53$

Thus, 2 tens 3 ones < 53 ones.

B. Two hundred and two = 202

One hundred and two = 102

Since, $202 > 102$

So, two hundred and two > one hundred and two

C. $200 + 60 + 3 = 263 \Rightarrow 200 + 70 = 270$

Since, $263 < 270$

So, $200 + 60 + 3 < 200 + 70$

D. 72 tens $= 72 \times 10 = 720$

$\Rightarrow 700 + 20 + 0 = 720$

Since, $720 = 720$

So, 72 tens $= 700 + 20 + 0$

Hence, A → < ; B → > ; C → < ; D → =

18. *(d)* After arranging the lost pages in increasing order, $1 < 4 < 6 < 8$

So, the correct order is $15 < 49 < 65 < 84$.

19. *(a)* The descending order of the given collection of the numbers is

$762 > 562 > 441 > 436 > 342 > 332 > 251 > 235$

Hence, option (a) is correct.

20. *(b)* The smallest possible 3-digit number formed by using the digits 8, 6, 4 is 468.

21. *(d)* Given that the sixth compartment of the train has 75 passengers.

22. *(c)* We know that, smallest 3-digit number $= 100$

So, the fifth compartment has 100 passengers.

23. *(b)* 1. False, there are 6 ones in 406.

2. True, since, smallest 3-digit number $= 100$ and $100 - 1 = 99$

3. True, 800 ones $= 800 \times 1 = 800$ and 80 tens $= 80 \times 10 = 800$

4. False, since largest 3-digit number formed using digits 9, 2, 5 is 952, which is an even number.

2. Addition and Subtraction

1. *(a)* Given, $342 + 124$

$$\begin{array}{r} \text{H} \quad \text{T} \quad \text{O} \\ 3 \quad 4 \quad 2 \\ + \ 1 \quad 2 \quad 4 \\ \hline 4 \quad 6 \quad 6 \end{array}$$

2. *(b)* Given, $49 + 36$

$$\begin{array}{r} 4 \quad 9 \\ + \ 3 \quad 6 \\ \hline 8 \quad 5 \end{array}$$

Spet I : First add, $9 + 6 = 15$ write 5 in ones and carry over 1 to the tens place.

Step II : Now, add $1 + 4 + 3 = 8$

So, the sum of 49 and 36 is 85.

3. *(b)* Given, $m + n = 460$

In option (a), $208 + 295 = 503 \neq 460$

In option (b), $196 + 264 = 460$

In option (c), $156 + 178 = 334 \neq 460$

In option (d), $352 + 109 = 461 \neq 460$

$\therefore \qquad m = 196$ and $n = 264$

Hence, option (b) is correct.

4. *(b)* $\therefore$ Total number of hours Vinay watched TV in a week $= 3 + 2 + 4 + 2 + 2 + 5 + 0 = 18$

5. *(b)* Violet $\rightarrow$ $7 + 14 = 21$
    Indigo $\rightarrow$ $6 + 13 = 19$
    Blue $\rightarrow$ $5 + 12 = 17$
    Green $\rightarrow$ $4 + 11 = 15$
    Yellow $\rightarrow$ $3 + 10 = 13$
    Orange $\rightarrow$ $2 + 9 = 11$
    Red $\rightarrow$ $1 + 8 = 9$

So, orange has the second lowest sum. i.e., 11.

6. *(a)* Amount of money in Raju's one pocket
$$= ₹\, 24$$
Amount of money in Raju's another pocket
$$= ₹\, 39$$
$\therefore$ Total amount of money $= ₹\, 24 + ₹\, 39 = ₹\, 63$

7. *(d)* Number of pencils bought on Friday $= 167$
Number of pencils bought on Sunday $= 234$
Number of pencils bought on Tuesday $= 371$
$\therefore$ Total pencils bought by Anjali
$$= 167 + 234 + 371 = 772$$

8. *(d)* The pattern is as follows
Sum of the numbers in the bottom three boxes $=$ Number on the top box
i.e., $\qquad 240 + 130 + 115 = 485$
and $\qquad 105 + 382 + 436 = 923$
Similarly, $195 + 218 + 533 = 946$
So, the missing number is 946.

9. *(c)*   Total number of pages $= 87$
   Number of pages left to read $= -24$
Number of pages already read $= 63$

10. *(c)* Given, $849 - 267$

H	T	O
8	8	9
$-\ 2$	6	7
6	2	2

11. *(d)* Given, $75 - 27$

T	O
7	5
$-\ 2$	7
4	8

Step I : First take carry from tens place, then ones place digit become 15.

Now, subtract $15 - 7 = 8$

Step II : After giving carry tens place become 6.

Now subtract 2 from $6 = 6 - 2 = 4$

So, the subtraction of 75 and 27 is 48.

12. *(d)* First abacus 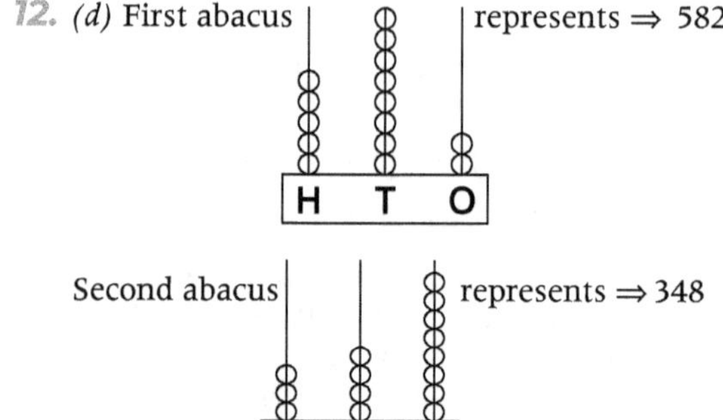 represents $\Rightarrow 582$

Second abacus represents $\Rightarrow 348$

So, $582 - 348 = 234$

13. *(b)* Number of passengers in train $= 927$
Number of passengers deboard at first station
$$= 369$$
Remaining passengers in train
$$= 927 - 369 = 558$$

14. *(b)* Largest 3-digit odd number $= 999$
and smallest 3- digit number $= 100$
So, difference $=$ Largest 3-digit odd number
$$\qquad - \text{Smallest 3-digit number}$$
$$= 999 - 100$$
$$= 899$$

15. *(b)* It is given that, each sister got 3 pencils and there are 9 pencils in total.
So,

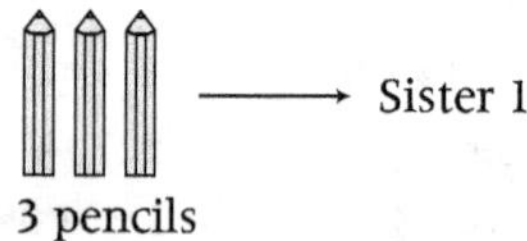

Remaining pencils $= 9 - 3 = 6$

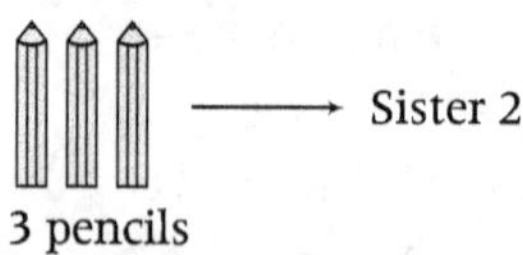

Remaining pencils = 6 – 3 = 3

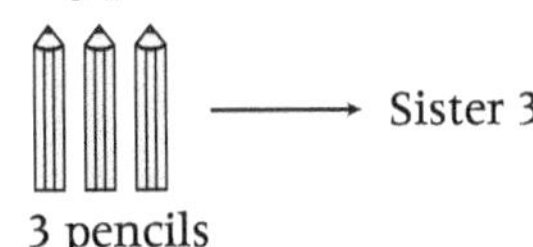

Remaining pencils = 3 – 3 = 0
So, George has 3 sisters.

16. *(a)* The pattern is as follows:
Subtraction of the number in the upper triangle = Number on bottom triangle
i.e., $485 - 269 = 216$ and
$750 - 399 = 351$
Similarly, $677 - 345 = \boxed{332}$
So, the missing number is 332.

17. *(d)* Number of benches in classroom 7 and 9
$= 37 + 46 = 83$

18. *(b)* Number of benches in classroom 7 = 37
Number of benches in classroom 8 = 29
Number of benches in class 7 is less than class 8 = $37 - 29 = 8$

19. *(d)* Option (a) is correct.
$150 + 245 = 395$
Option (b) is correct.
$500 - 105 = 495 = 395$
So, option (c) is correct.
$195 + 200 = 395$
Option (d) is incorrect.
$\because \quad 1000 - 505 = 495 \neq 395$

20. *(b)* Given, $A = 100 + 173 = 273$
$B = 250 + 34 = 284;$
$C = 500 - 237 = 263$
and $\quad D = 500 - 216 = 284$
So, option (b) is correct.
Hence, B and D have equal values.

21. *(a)* Given, $\triangle = 49$, $\square = 38$
Then, $\triangle + \triangle = 49 + 49 = 98$
$\therefore \triangle + \triangle - \square = 98 - 38 = 60$
Hence, option (a) is correct.

22. *(a)* If we add 8 and 4 and subtract 2 from it, then the result will be maximum.
i.e., $\quad 8 + 4 = 12$
and $\quad 12 - 2 = 10$

23. *(b)* The sum of the numbers written on school bag is $83 + 47 + 71 + 36 = 237$

24. *(c)* 21 is put into machine.
Add $15 \to 21 + 15 = 36$
Subtract $9 \to 36 - 9 = 27$
Add $37 \to 27 + 37 = 64$
Subtract $20 \to 64 - 20 = 44$
Hence, option (c) is correct.

25. *(d)* Option (d), $8 + 4 = 12$ and $16 - 4 = 12$
$\therefore \quad\quad\quad 12 = 12$
Hence, option (d) is correct.

3. Multiplication

1. *(c)* We know, $0 \times 1 \times 2 = 0$
[any number multiplied by zero becomes zero]

2. *(a)* We have,

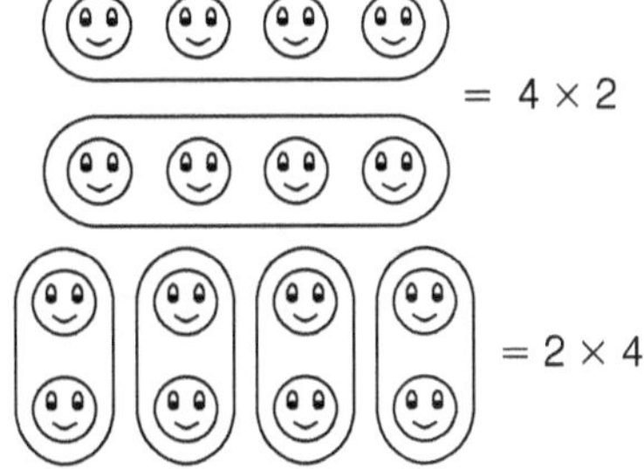

So, two multiplication sentences are 4×2 and 2×4.
Hence, option (a) is correct.

3. *(a)* Number of players = 9
Number of runs made by each player = 30
Total number of runs = $9 \times 30 = 270$
So, option (a) is correct.

4. *(d)* Number of sides 1 pentagon has = 5
Number of sides 5 pentagon has = $5 \times 5 = 25$
Hence, option (d) is correct.

5. *(d)* The given tadpole is on number 8 and we know that, $4 \times 2 = 8$, $2 \times 4 = 8$, $1 \times 8 = 8$
So, either 4 jumps of 2 or 2 jumps of 4 or 1 jump of 8 will make the frog to reach his tadpole.

6. *(a)* As given in question, note = ₹ 50
Number of notes = 7

Total money = ₹50 × 7 = ₹ 350

So, option (a) is correct.

7. *(d)* By the given question picture,

Number of legs of 1 spider = 8

Pair of legs of 1 spider = 4

[∵ pair means 2 and 4 × 2 = 8]

∴ Pairs of legs of 8 spider = 4 × 8 = 32

8. *(b)* Number of apples hanging on each tree = 18

Number of trees = 9

Total number of apples = 18 × 9 = 162

Hence, option (b) is correct.

9. *(c)* Number of boys = 24

Number of girls = 36

Total number of students = 36 + 24 = 60

Number of classes = 8

Total students in 8 classes = 8 × 60 = 480

Hence, option (c) is correct.

10. *(d)*

1. $\underline{8} \times 5 = 40$
2. $934 \times \underline{1} = 934$
3. ∵ Smallest even number = 2

∴ 2 times of the smallest even number

$$= 2 \times 2 = \underline{4}$$

4. $9 \times 10 = \underline{90}$

So, 1 → B; 2 → D; 3 → A; 4 → C

11. *(b)*

1. There are $\underline{5}$ 7's in 35.   [∵ 5 × 7 = 35]
2. 25 tens × 2 ones = 25 × 10 × 25 × 1

$$= \underline{500}$$

3. Number of children in a class = 4

Number of toffees eaten by each child = 5

∴ They ate (5 × 4) = $\underline{20}$ toffees in all.

4. 8 group of 4 is equal to 8 × 4 = $\underline{32}$

$$= 78 - 34 = \underline{44}$$

12. *(a)* Given, ⊢—⊣ = 3 steps

Distance between Misha's house and a nearby park = 7⊢—⊣

$$= 7 \times 3 \text{ steps} = 21 \text{ steps}$$

So, Misha will have to move 21 steps in order to reach park from her house.

13. *(c)* Given,

<table>
<tr><td></td><td>7</td><td>8</td></tr>
<tr><td>3</td><td>A</td><td>B</td></tr>
<tr><td>4</td><td>C</td><td>D</td></tr>
</table>

On multiply the numbers in each row and column, we get

A = 3 × 7 or 7 × 3 = 21

B = 3 × 8 or 8 × 3 = 24

C = 4 × 7 or 7 × 4 = 28

D = 4 × 8 or 8 × 4 = 32

∴ A = 21, B = 24, C = 28 and D = 32

14. *(c)* Given,   1 bell = 12

and   1 cap + 3 bells = 57

⇒   1 cap + 3 × 12 = 57

⇒   1 cap + 36 = 57

⇒   1 cap = 57 − 36

⇒   1 cap = 21

Also, 3 caps + 1 paper clip = 70

⇒   3 × 21 + 1 paper clip = 70   [∵ 1 cap = 21]

⇒   63 + 1 paper clip = 70

∴   1 paper clip = 70 − 63 = 7

15. *(a)* From the given figure, it is clear that there are 8 steps on each staircase.

and floor on which Mary stays = Thirteenth

∴ Number of steps Mary has to climb to reach her floor = 4 × Number of steps on each staircase = 13 × 8 = 104

16. *(c)* Quantity of guavas = 4 kg

Rate of guavas = ₹ 40 per kg

So, cost of guavas = 4 kg × ₹ 40 = ₹ 160

Quantity of mangoes = 3 kg

Rate of mangoes = ₹ 25 per kg

So, cost of mangoes = 3 kg × ₹ 25 = ₹ 75

∴ Total cost = ₹ 160 + ₹ 75 = ₹ 235

17. *(d)* Number of trays bought from market

$$= 4 \text{ dozen} = 4 \times 12 = 48$$

Number of defective trays = 5

Number of trays broke down = 15

So, total number of defective trays

$$= (15 + 5) = 20$$

∴ Number of good trays left = 48 − 20 = 28

18. *(a)* Given, number of girls in each group = 6

Number of girls in in 4 group $= 6 \times 4 = 24$

6 girls wals into the hall and join them

So, total number of girls in hall = 24 + 6 = 30

19. *(c)* Given, number of boys in each section = 15

Number of boys in 7 sections $15 \times 7 = 105$

Number of boys were absent = 30

So, total number of boys were present

$$= 105 - 30 = 75$$

20. *(b)* Given, number of kinder joy sold on saturday = 20

Then, number of kinder joy sold on Sunday

$$= 3 \times 20 = 60$$

Number of kinder joy sold on Wednesday

$$= 4 \times 60 = 240$$

So, total number of kinder joy sold on Sunday and wednesday both

$$= 60 + 240 = 300$$

4. Division

1. *(d)* As we know,

$$7) \boxed{?} (2$$
$$\underline{14}$$
$$5$$

If 14 is subtracted from any number and result will be 5, then, the number is

14 + 5 = 19

Hence, option (d) is correct.

2. *(a)* If we observe the question then we get, there is a division of 3.

i.e., $\dfrac{21}{7} = 3, \dfrac{12}{4} = 3, \dfrac{18}{6} = 3$

Similarly, $\dfrac{\boxed{15}}{5} = 3$

Hence, option (a) is correct.

3. *(d)* Number of children in Mrs. Bhaskar's music school = 48

Number of groups = 6

∴ Number of children in each group

$$= 48 \div 6 = 8$$

4. *(d)* Number of stars = 3

3 ☆ = 12 stickers.

1 ☆ = 12 ÷ 3 = 4 stickers

Now, ☆ ☆ ☆ ☆ ☆ $= 4 \times 5 = 20$

Hence, option (d) is correct.

5. *(d)* Total number of bananas = 18

Number of children = 3

∴ Number of bananas each child will get

$$= 18 \div 3 = 6$$

6. *(b)* Number of pens Virat has = 12

Number of pens each sister got = 3

∴ Number of sisters = Number of pens ÷ Number of pens each sister got = 12 ÷ 3 = 4

7. *(c)* Capacity of bucket = 54 literes

Capacity of glass = 3 literes

∴ Number of glasses will poured = 54 ÷ 3 = 18

8. *(a)* Total beads = 8

Number of sticks = 2

Tim divides 8 beads equally between 2 sticks.

∴ Number of beads in each sticks = 8 ÷ 2 = 4

9. *(b)* Total number of chairs = 81

Number of rows = 9

∴ Number of chairs in each row = 81 ÷ 9 = 9

10. *(b)* Number of days Kareena has = 7

Number of pages book contain = 52

Then, $7) 52 (7$
$$\underline{49}$$
$$3$$

So, 3 pages is left to read. Hence, option (b) is correct.

11. *(b)* Number of girls = 24

Number of boys = 21

Total number of students = 24 + 21 = 45

Number of groups formed by them = 5

∴ Number of children in each group

$$= 45 \div 5 = 9$$

12. *(a)* Number of chocolates = 21

Number of boys = 7

∴ Number of chocolates each boy will get

$$= 21 \div 7 = 3$$

So, number of chocolates 4 boys will get

$$= 3 \times 4 = 12$$

Hence, option (a) is correct.

13. *(a)* Number of chocolates Akshay has = 72

Number of friends = 4

∴ Number of chocolates each friend will get
$$= 72 \div 4 = 18$$

14. *(a)* Number of candles in a pack = 5

Total candles = 30

∴ Number of packs = 30 ÷ 5 = 6

15. *(b)* Total bill of shikanji = ₹ 64

∴ Number of friends = 8

They want to share the bill equally.

∴ Share of each = 64 ÷ 8 = ₹ 8

16. *(d)* Total number of gifts = 36

Total persons = Gaurav + 2 friends = 3

∴ Number of gifts packed by each person
$$= 36 \div 3 = 12$$

17. *(c)* Total number of mangoes = 42

Number of rotten mangoes = 9

Number of mangoes left = 42 − 9 = 33

Capacity of each bag = 3

∴ Number of bags = 33 ÷ 3 = 11

18. *(d)* Number of toy cars Akansha has = 36

Number of rows = 6

Number of toy cars in each row = 36 ÷ 6 = 6

If she want to arrange them in 8 rows then

Total number of toy cars = Number of toy cars in each row × Number of rows = 6 × 8 = 48

∴ Number of toy cars more than previous
$$= 48 − 36 = 12$$

Hence, option (d) is correct.

19. *(a)*

1. False, Any number divided by the number itself gives 1.
2. True, Any number divided by 1 given the number itself.
3. False, cost of 2 table = ₹400

   ∴ Cost of 1 table = 400 ÷ 2 = ₹200 ≠ ₹ 190
4. False, The number that we are dividing by is called divisor.

5. Measurement

1. *(b)* We know that the measurements on a scale starts from 0.

So, the length of the scale is 7 centimetres as shown below:

2. *(a)* The measurement of the length of cassette starts from 6 inches and goes upto 10 inches.

∴ Length of the cassette = 10 − 6 = 4 inches

3. *(a)* Given, Distance between Delhi and Agra
$$= 243 \text{ km}$$

and distance between Agra and Jaipur
$$= 356 \text{ km}$$

Now, Distance between Delhi and Jaipur

= Distance between Delhi and Agra

+ Distance between Agra and Jaipur

= 243 km + 356 km

= 599 km

4. *(d)* Sunny is at the starting point.

Distance between Sunny and Jonny
$$= 76 \text{ metres}$$

Distance between Jonny and Kunal
$$= 46 \text{ metres}$$

Distance between Kunal and finish line
$$= 28 \text{ metres}$$

∴ Total distance that Sunny needs to run
$$= 76 + 46 + 28 = 150 \text{ metres}$$

5. *(a)* Height of coconut tree = 43 metres

Height of wooden block = 15 metres

∴ Height of Monku need to jump

= Height of coconut tree

− Height of wooden block

= 43 − 15 = 28 metres

6. *(c)* Length of one piece of rope
$$= 12 \text{ centimetres}$$

Number of pieces joined = 5

∴ Length of the larger rope formed
$$= 5 \times 12 = 60 \text{ centimetres}$$

7. *(b)* Length of pencil A $= 9 - 2 = 7$ centimetres
Length of pencil B $= 5 - 0 = 5$ centimetres
Length of pencil C $= 11 - 6 = 5$ centimetres
Length of pencil D $= 10 - 4 = 6$ centimetres
So, the length of the longest pencil is
7 centimetres.

8. *(b)* Given,

In Box A,   **In Box B,**
$\Delta = 4\,$kg $O = 3\,$kg
$\therefore \Delta\,\Delta = 4 + 4 = 8\,$kg; $\therefore OOO = 3 + 3 + 3 = 9\,$kg
So, on comparing,
Box B is heavier than Box A.
Option (b) is correct.

9. *(c)* As per the diagram,
Weight of Zoya and puppy $= 65$ kilograms
and weight of puppy $= 4$ kilograms
$\therefore$ Weight of Zoya $=$ Weight of Zoya and puppy
$$- \text{Weight of puppy}$$
$$= 65 - 4 = 61 \text{ kilograms}$$

10. *(b)* Given, $1\,O = 7$ grams
The diagram has $9\,O$.
Then, $\quad 9\,O = 9 \times 7 = 63$ grams
Given, Weight of $9\,O =$ Weight of box
$\therefore \qquad$ Weight of box $= 63$ grams

11. *(c)* Given, weight of Saira $= 35$ kilograms
$\therefore$ Weight of Beth
$$= \text{Weight of Saira} - 7 \text{ kilograms}$$
$[\because$ Beth is 7 kilograms lighter than Saira$]$
$$= 35 - 7 = 28 \text{ kilograms}$$
and Adira is 10 kilograms heavier than Beth.
$\therefore$ Weight of Adira $=$ Weight of Beth
$$+ 10 \text{ kilograms}$$
$$= 28 + 10$$
$$= 38 \text{ kilograms}$$

12. *(d)* According to the question,
Mango $+ 250$ gm $= 100$ gm $+ 100$ gm
$$+ 100 \text{ gm} + 100 \text{ gm} + 50 \text{ gm} = 450 \text{ gm}$$
$\therefore$ Mango $= 450$ gm $- 250$ gm
$\therefore$ Mango $= 200$ gm
So, After calculating, the weight of Mango is
200 gm.

13. *(d)* From the given diagrams,
Weight of a pineapple $= 220$ grams
Weight of an apple $= 150$ grams
Weight of a mango $= 170$ grams
$\therefore$ Difference between the weights of a
pineapple and a mango $= 220 - 170$
$$= 50 \text{ grams}$$

14. *(d)* When a mango is placed on machine B,
then weight on machine B $= 150 + 170$
$$= 320 \text{ grams}$$
According to the given diagram,
Weight on machine A $= 220$ grams
Weight on machine C $= 170$ grams
So, it is clear that weight on machine C is
least and weight on machine B is greatest.
Hence, option (d) is correct.

15. *(b)* Arranging the volume in ascending order,
we get
8 litre and 345 mL $<$ 9 litre and 100 mL
$$< 11 \text{ litre} < 12 \text{ litre and } 726 \text{ mL}$$

So, 12 litre and 726 millilitres is the greatest
quantity of water contained in container B.
[Here, '$<$' sign indicates greater than.]

16. *(b)* Volume of water required on Monday
$$= 150 \text{ litres}$$
Volume of water required on Tuesday
$$= 243 \text{ litres}$$
Volume of water required on Wednesday
$$= 182 \text{ litres}$$
$\therefore$ Total volume of water required by factory in
all the three days $= 150 + 243 + 182$
$$= 575 \text{ litres}$$

17. *(b)* Volume of water drink in each day
$$= 3 \text{ litres}$$
Number of days in 2 weeks $= 2 \times$ Number of
days in a week $= 2 \times 7 = 14$ days
$\therefore$ Volume of water drink in 14 days
$$= 14 \times 3 = 42 \text{ litres}$$

18. *(c)* Volume of tank $= 45$ litres
Volume of bucket $= 5$ litres
Volume of tank filled by 1 bucket $= 5$ litres

Volume of tank filled by 2 buckets
$$= 2 \times 5 = 10 \text{ litres and so on.}$$
∴ Volume of tank filled by 9 buckets
$$= 9 \times 5 = 45 \text{ litres}$$
So, 9 buckets of water are required to fill the tank completely.

19. *(d)* Total volume of water required by Greta while doing all household work
$$= 15 + 50 + 40 = 105 \text{ litres}$$
Total volume of water required by Greta's mother while doing all household work
$$= 10 + 40 + 30 = 80 \text{ litres}$$
∴ Volume of extra water used by Greta
$$= 105 - 80 = 25 \text{ litres}$$

20. *(d)* Given, temperature on thermometer $= 67°C$
So, the room temperature = temperature in thermometer $- 19°C$
[∵ Room temperature is 19°C less than from temperature in thermometer]
$$= 67°C - 19°C = 48°C$$

21. *(d)* 1. The weight of a sack of sugar is about 20 kilograms.
    2. The length of the door is about 2 metres.
    3. The volume of beaker is about 7 litres.
    4. The volume of a glass is about 300 millilitres.
So, $1 \rightarrow B; 2 \rightarrow A; 3 \rightarrow D; 4 \rightarrow C$

6. Money

1. *(a)* We know that,
$$1 \text{ rupee} = 100 \text{ paise}$$
then, 25 paise + 25 paise + 25 paise + 25 paise
$$= 100 \text{ paise} = 1 \text{ rupee}$$
Hence, four, 25 paise coins makes a rupee.

2. *(d)* We know that, ₹1 = 100 paise
$$\Rightarrow \quad ₹5 = 5 \times 100 \text{ paise} = 500 \text{ paise}$$
∴ Total paise received by Lero
$$= 25 \text{ paise} + 100 \text{ paise} + 50 \text{ paise} + 500 \text{ paise}$$
$$= 675 \text{ paise}$$

3. *(d)* Cost of a can of juice $= ₹65$
In option (a), ₹50 + ₹10 + ₹20 + ₹5 = ₹85
In option (b), ₹50 + ₹ 20 = ₹70

In option (c), ₹20 + ₹20 + ₹50 = ₹90
In option (d), ₹50 + ₹10 + ₹5 = ₹65
Since, machine requires exact change. So, money in option (d) should be put in.

4. *(a)* 1. Savings of Kate $= ₹10 + ₹10 + ₹20 = ₹40$
    2. Savings of Zeena
$$= ₹20 + ₹10 + ₹5 + ₹5 + ₹20 = ₹60$$
    3. Savings of Amira
$$= ₹20 + ₹5 + ₹2 + ₹2 + ₹1 = ₹30$$
    4. Savings of Brad
$$= ₹10 + ₹20 + ₹5 + ₹5 + ₹10 = ₹50$$
So, $1 \rightarrow D; 2 \rightarrow C; 3 \rightarrow B; 4 \rightarrow A$

5. *(a)* In option (a), ₹1 + ₹5 + 25 paise
$$= ₹6 + 25 \text{ paise}$$
$$= 6 \text{ rupees and 25 paise}$$
[rupees are added to rupees and paise are added to paise]
In option (b),
$$25 \text{ paise} + 50 \text{ paise} + 10 \text{ paise} = 85 \text{ paise}$$
In option (c),
$$₹2 + ₹1 + 50 \text{ paise} + 50 \text{ paise}$$
$$= ₹3 + 100 \text{ paise}$$
$$= ₹3 + ₹1 \qquad [∵ 100 \text{ paise} = ₹1]$$
$$= ₹4$$
So, the greatest amount is shown by option (a).

6. *(c)* Cost of a frock (A) $= ₹55$
Cost of a purse (B) $= ₹250$
Cost of a pair of shoes (C) $= ₹80$
Cost of a necklace (D) $= ₹100$
After arranging the items from the most expensive to the most cheapest, we get
$$B, D, C, A$$
Hence, option (c) is correct.

7. *(d)* Cost of a pencil box $= ₹20$
Cost of a book $= ₹32.50$
∴ Total cost = Cost of a pencil box + Cost of a book $= ₹20 + ₹32.50 = ₹52.50$

8. *(c)* Number of chocolates that can be bought for ₹10 = 3
So, number of chocolates that can be bought for ₹10 + ₹10 + ₹10 $= ₹30 = 3 + 3 + 3 = 9$

9. *(c)* Cost of a pencil = 30 paise

Cost of a sharpener = 50 paise

Cost of an eraser = 45 paise

Cost of a ruler = 35 paise

In option (c),

Total cost of a sharpener and a ruler

$$= 50 \text{ paise} + 35 \text{ paise} = 85 \text{ paise}$$

So, Greta can buy a sharpener and a ruler with 85 paise.

10. *(c)* Cost of a purse = ₹ 450

Change received = ₹ 235

∴ Total money Kaira paid

$$= \text{Cost of a purse} + \text{Change received}$$
$$= ₹\,450 + ₹\,235 = ₹\,685$$

11. *(b)* Prabhat has = ₹ 12.75

Cost of chocolate = ₹ 5

So, remaining money

$$= ₹\,12.75 - ₹\,5 = ₹\,7.75$$

12. *(d)* Cost of a hamburger = ₹ 28

Cost of a cookie = ₹ 45

∴   Total cost = ₹ 45 + ₹ 28 = ₹ 73

Amount of coupon = ₹ 10

∴ Total money Simone have to pay

$$= \text{Total cost} - \text{Amount of coupon}$$
$$= ₹\,73 - ₹\,10 = ₹\,63$$

13. *(b)* Jorg had = ₹ 524

Money given by Yura to Jorg = ₹ 113

∴ Total money Jorg have now = ₹ 524 + ₹113

$$= ₹\,637$$

Money given by Jorg to his friend = ₹ 192

So, money left with Jorg = ₹ 637 − ₹192

$$= ₹\,445$$

14. *(b)* Number of apples Suzanne had = 32

Number of apples in 1 packet = 4

Since, $4 \times 8 = 32$

Thus, 32 apples must be packed in 8 packets.

Cost of 1 packet = ₹ 12

∴ Cost of 8 packets = ₹12 × 8 = ₹ 96

15. *(a)* Cost of a winter cap

$$= ₹\,2 \text{ tens and } 20 \text{ ones}$$

$$= ₹\,(2 \times 10 + 20 \times 1)$$
$$= ₹\,(20 + 20) = ₹\,40$$

In option (a), ₹ 5 tens = ₹ 5 × 10 = ₹ 50

Hence, option (a) is correct.

16. *(c)* Cost of 1 corn muffin = ₹ 2

Cost of 7 corn muffins = 7 × ₹ 2 = ₹14

Cost of 1 blueberry muffins = ₹ 3

Cost of 9 blueberry muffins = 9 × ₹ 3 = ₹ 27

∴ Total cost of 7 corn muffins and 9 blueberry muffins = ₹14 + ₹ 27 = ₹41

17. *(c)* Number of hours between 7 : 00 pm and 12 mid-night = 12 mid-night – 7 : 00 pm = 5 hours

It is given that taxi charges ₹ 15 extra for every hour after 7 : 00 pm.

∴ Extra money which Kim and his family had to pay = ₹15× Number of hours between 7 : 00 pm and 12 mid-night = ₹15 × 5 = ₹ 75

18. *(b)* 1. True, five 10 paise coins = 5 × 10 paise

$$= 50 \text{ paise}$$

2. False, four 2 paise coins + one 1 paise coin

$$= 4 \times 2 \text{ paise} + 1 \times 1 \text{ paise} \neq 10 \text{ paise}$$
$$= 8 + 1 \text{ paise} = 9 \text{ paise} \neq 10 \text{ paise}$$

3. True, Kina has = ₹ 35

Gianne has = ₹ 40

∴   Total money = ₹ 40 + ₹ 35 = ₹ 75

4. True, cost of 1 banana = ₹ 6

∴   Cost of 12 bananas = ₹ 6 × 12 = ₹ 72

19. *(b)* 1. ∵   ₹ 1 = 100 paise

∴ 2 rupees = 2 × 100 paise = 200 paise

So, there are <u>200</u> paise in ₹ 2.

2. Since, 2 × 50 paise = 100 paise = ₹ 1

So, <u>2</u> , 50 paise coins make a ₹ 1

3. Since, ₹ 28 + ₹ <u>72</u> = ₹100

So, ₹ <u>72</u> should be added to ₹ 28 to get ₹ 100.

4. Cost of 1 pen = ₹ 15

Cost of 1 book = ₹ 55

∴   Total cost = ₹ 55 + ₹15 = ₹ 70

So, 1 pen costs ₹ 15 and 1 book costs ₹ 55, then the total cost in ₹ <u>70</u>.

Hence, option (b) is correct.

20. *(c)* Cost of 1 kiwi fruit = 24 paise

Cost of 2 kiwi fruits = 2 × 24 paise = 48 paise

Cost of 1 kilogram strawberries = 21 paise

Cost of 3 kilograms strawberries = 3 × 21 paise
$$= 63 \text{ paise}$$

Cost of 1 banana = 18 paise

Cost of 4 bananas = 4 × 18 paise = 72 paise

∴ Total cost = 48 paise + 63 paise + 72 paise
$$= 183 \text{ paise}$$

Total money given
$$= ₹5 = 5 \times 100 \text{ paise}$$
$$= 500 \text{ paise} \quad [∵ ₹1 = 100 \text{ paise}]$$

∴ Required change = 500 paise − 183 paise
$$= 317 \text{ paise}$$

Hence, option (c) is correct.

21. *(d)* In option (d),

Cost of 1 kilogram raspberries = 34 paise

Cost of 2 kilograms raspberries = 2 × 34 paise
$$= 68 \text{ paise}$$

Cost of a pineapple = 47 paise

∴ Total cost of 2 kilograms raspberries and a pineapple = 68 paise + 47 paise = 115 paise

So, items in option (d) are the most expensive.

22. *(b)* Total number of members = 5

Age of Misi = 3 years

Age of Misi's sister = Age of Misi + 3 years
$$= 3 \text{ years} + 3 \text{ years} = 6 \text{ years}$$

Age of Misi's brother = Age of Misi + 8 years
$$= 3 \text{ years} + 8 \text{ years}$$
$$= 11 \text{ years}$$

From the given table,

Cost of ticket for Misi = Free

Cost of ticket for Misi's sister = ₹8

Cost of ticket for Misi's brother = ₹8

Cost of ticket for Misi's father = ₹18

Cost of ticket for Misi's mother = ₹18

∴ Total cost of tickets
$$= ₹8 + ₹8 + ₹18 + ₹18 = ₹52$$

7. Time and Calendar

1. *(d)* According to the question, hour hand is between 5 and 6 and minute hand is at 6.

Thus, the time is 5 : 30.

2. *(c)*

At 12 : 30, the hour hand is between 12 and 1.

3. *(d)* The time shown by the arrow is 3 O'clock.

So, it can be either 3 : 00 pm or 3 : 00 am.

4. *(b)* 23 : 30 = 11 : 30 am + 12 hours
$$= 11 : 30 \text{ in the night}$$

5. *(b)* Minute hand is at 12 once in every hour i.e., at 12 : 00 am, 1 : 00 am, 2 : 00 am, 3 : 00 am,

4 : 00 am, 5 : 00 am, 6 : 00 am, 7 : 00 am,

8 : 00 am, 9 : 00 am, 10 : 00 am, 11 : 00 am,

12 : 00 pm, 1 : 00 pm, 2 : 00 pm, 3 : 00 pm,

4 : 00 pm, 5 : 00 pm, 6 : 00 pm, 7 : 00 pm,

8 : 00 pm, 9 : 00 pm, 10 : 00 pm, 11 : 00 pm.

So, 24 times in a day, the minute hand is at 12.

6. *(d)* 30 seconds + 30 seconds + 30 seconds
$$= 90 \text{ seconds} = 1 \text{ minute } 30 \text{ seconds}$$

Hence, option (d) is correct.

7. *(c)* As we studied that,

1 hour = 60 minutes

So, 48 hours = 48 × 60 minutes
$$= 2880 \text{ minutes}.$$

8. *(d)* Total time needed to feed each cow one by one = 10 minutes + 20 minutes + 16 minutes
$$+ \ 12 \text{ minutes} = 58 \text{ minutes}$$

9. *(a)* Office timings of Kara
$$= 9 : 00 \text{ am to} - 5 : 00 \text{ pm}$$
Number of hours between 9 : 00 am to 5 : 00 pm = 8 hours
Lunch break = 1 hour
∴ Total working time of Kara
$$= 8 \text{ hours} - 1 \text{ hour} = 7 \text{ hours}$$

10. *(b)* Take off time of flight = 4 : 00 pm
Flying time = 2 hours and 20 minutes
∴ Landing time = 4 : 00 pm
$$+ \ 2 \text{ hours } 20 \text{ minutes}$$
$$= 6 : 20 \text{ pm}$$

11. *(a)* Given, bank opens at 7 : 30 am.
Time at which Elia arrived at the bank
$$= 7 : 10 \text{ am}$$
∴ Waiting time of Elia = 7 : 30 am − 7 : 10 am
$$= 20 \text{ minutes}$$

12. *(c)* The clock shows 8 : 30 pm.
Given that, Tabbu can watch TV only till 10 : 00 pm.
∴ Remaining time = 10 : 00 pm − 8 : 30 pm
$$= 1 \text{ hour } 30 \text{ minutes}$$

13. *(d)* It is 6 O'clock in the watch.
Sara is moving the hands by half an hour and then by 1 hour and then repeats the same pattern.
So, we have

$6 : 00 \rightarrow 6 : 30 \rightarrow 7 : 30 \rightarrow 8 : 00 \rightarrow 9 : 00 \rightarrow$

30 minutes   1 hour   30 minutes   1 hour   30 minutes

$12 : 00 \leftarrow 11 : 00 \leftarrow 10 : 30 \leftarrow 9 : 30$

1 hour   30 minutes   1 hour

So, in 8 turns, the time will be exactly 12 O'clock.

14. *(b)* Time taken by sand to come from top to bottom in 1 turn = 30 minutes.
∴ Time taken by sand to come from top to bottom in 5 turns = 5 × 30 minutes
$$= 150 \text{ minutes} = 2 \text{ hours } 30 \text{ minutes}$$

15. *(d)* Time at which Simplon-Orient Express depart from Toledo = 8 : 00 am
Travelling time = 6 hours
∴ Time at which Simplon-Orient Express arrives at Blackburn = 8 : 00 am + 6 hours
$$= 2 : 00 \text{ pm}$$
Time at which Eagle Danube Express depart from Toledo = 8 : 30 am
Travelling time = 4 : 30 hours
∴ Time at which Eagle Danube Express arrives at Blackburn = 8 : 30 am + 4 : 30 hours
$$= 1 : 00 \text{ pm}$$
Time at which Oriental Express depart from Toledo = 8 : 00 am
Travelling time = 5 hours
∴ Time at which Oriental Express arrives at Blackburn = 8 : 00 am + 5 hours = 1 : 00 pm
So, Lewis will not catch any of these train, since they reach Blackburn at 1 : 00 pm or 2 : 00 pm.

16. *(a)* Departure time from the platform of Toledo = 9 : 30 am
Travelling time = 5 hours
∴ Arriving time on the platform of Blackburn
$$= 9 : 30 \text{ am} + 5 \text{ hours}$$
$$= 2 : 30 \text{ pm}$$

17. *(b)* It is given that Alka's school finishes off at 3'O clock in the afternoon and she requires 30 minutes to reach her home.
So, Alka reaches her home at 3 : 30 in the afternoon.
Now, one day she got 10 minutes late.
∴ Time at which Alka reached her home
$$= 3 : 30 \text{ pm} + 10 \text{ minutes}$$
$$= 3 : 40 \text{ pm}$$

At 3 : 40, the minute hand is at 8.
Hence, option (b) is correct.

18. *(c)* We know that, 1 hour = 60 minutes

$$1 \text{ day} = 24 \text{ hours}$$
$$1 \text{ week} = 7 \text{ days}$$
$$1 \text{ month} = 4 \text{ or } 5 \text{ weeks}$$

∴ Minute < Hour < Day < Week < Month

19. *(c)* 29th February comes after every four years.

[only a leap year has 29 days in February]

So, Kavya will celebrate her birthday after every four years.

20. *(a)* Number of days in a week = 7

Number of days in February = 28

Since, $7 \times 4 = 28$

So, the number of days in February is 4 times the number of days in a week.

21. *(a)* There are 5 Sunday in the given month i.e., 1st March, 8th March, 15th March, 22nd March and 29th March.

22. *(b)* Sara's exams starts from 2nd March.

Number of days in 1 week = 7

Number of days in 2 weeks = $7 \times 2 = 14$

∴ Sara's exams will be over on 15th March (2nd March + 14 days = 15 th March)

Now, number of days in March = 31

∴ Number of days Sara's vacations lasted

$$= 31 - 15 = 16$$

23. *(d)* As per the given calendar, National Voter's day is on 25th January.

Test of princy = 2 weeks before 25th January i.e., 14 days before 25th January.

∴, Date on which princy test has been scheduled = 25th January − 14 days

$$= 11\text{th January}$$

24. *(c)* In order to find the total number of days in a year, add the number of days in each month.

25. *(c)*

6th turn →	Monday	Tuesday	→ 3rd turn
	Wednesday	Thursday	→ 5th turn
2nd turn →	Friday	Saturday	→ 7th turn
4th turn →	Sunday	Holiday	→ 1st turn

So, after 7 turns, Wednesday is left without a cross mark.

26. *(c)*

1. **False**, the shortest hand of the clock is hour hand.

2. **True**,

3. **False**, 30 minutes after 5 : 30 is 6 : 00.

4. **True**, in May, there are 31 days. So, if 1 May is Sunday. So, there will be 5 Sunday in this month i.e., on 8th May, 15th May, 22nd May and 29th May.

27. *(c)*

1. 6 ten minutes = 6×10 minutes
$$= 60 \text{ minutes}$$
$$= \underline{1} \text{ hour}$$

2. There are <u>28</u> days in February in a non-leap year.

3. If today is Friday, then the day after six days will be <u>Thursday</u>.

[Saturday → Sunday → Monday

→ Tuesday → Wednesday → Thursday]

4. Seventh month of the year is <u>July</u>.

8. Shapes

1. *(c)* We know that quadrilateral has 4 sides. So, figure in option (c) is a quadrilateral. Hence, option (c) is correct.

2. *(b)* Option (b) The given solid is cube.

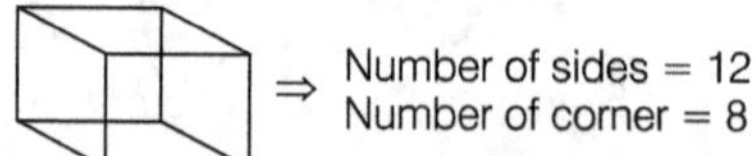

⇒ Number of sides = 12
Number of corner = 8

3. *(b)* Option (a) consists of cone, cube and cuboids.

Option (b) consists of cone, cylinder, cubes and cuboids.

Option (c) consists of cone, cuboid and cylinders.

Option (d) consists of cones, cube and cuboids.

So, only option figure (b) has maximum different types of 3-D shapes.

4. (c) The below figure has rectangles, circles and triangles but does not have any square.

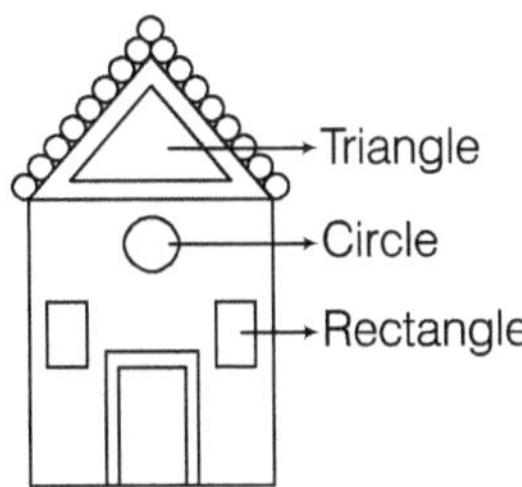

5. (a) A cylinder can be used to draw a circle.

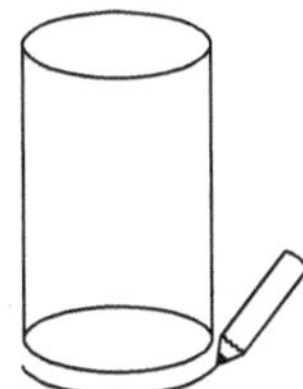

6. (a) The white patch on the football is a pentagon. Hence, option (a) is correct.

7. (d) Number of rectangular faces = 4

Number of square faces = 2

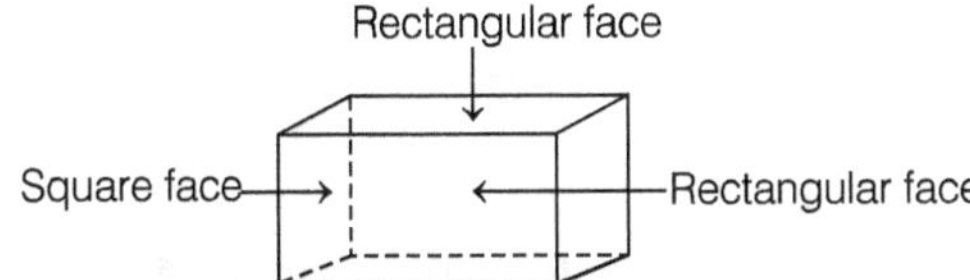

So, there are 2 less square faces than rectangular faces in solid given.
Hence, option (d) is correct.

8. (d) The figure is as follows:

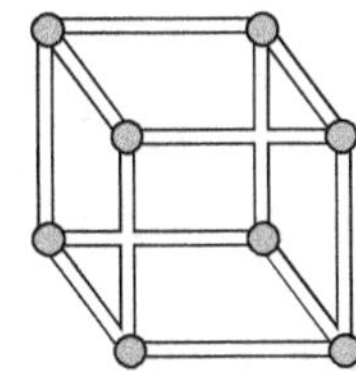

So, Sachin will need 12 straws and 8 balls of clay.

9. (b) It can be seen from the shapes chosen by Alisa that all the shapes are made up of straight lines.

10. (a) Out of the given letters, only three letters are made up of only straight lines, i.e., H, A, E.

11. (c) The given figure can be labelled as:

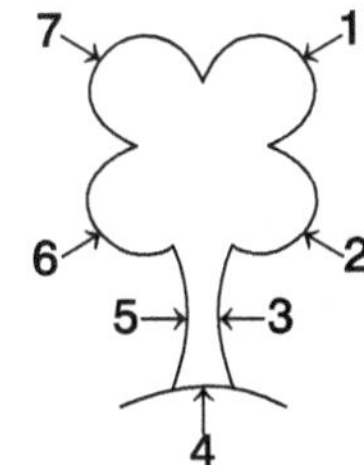

∴ So, the number of curved lines = 7

12. (a) Table for given figures is as follows:

Figure	Straight lines	Curved lines
A	2	2
B	8	0
C	1	2
D	0	2

Hence, only figure (A) has 2 straight lines and 2 curved lines.

13. (b) A. ▭ has 4 straight line.

B. △ has 3 straight line.

C. ◯ has 0 straight line.

D. ⌂ has 5 straight line.

So, A → 4; B → 3; C → 2; D → 1

Hence, option (b) is correct.

14. *(a)* The given figure can be labelled as:

So, the number of squares $= 11$

Hence, option (a) is correct.

15. *(b)* The given figure can be labelled as:

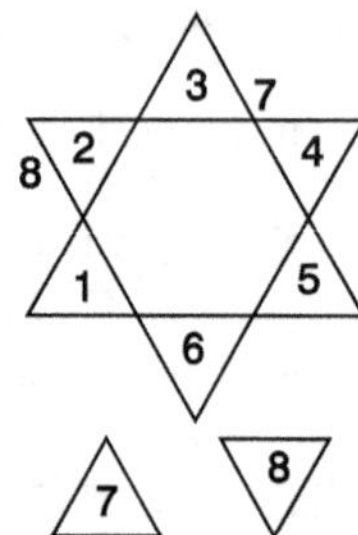

So, there are 8 triangles in the flag.

16. *(c)*

Figure	Number of sides
A	6
B	5
C	8
D	5

So, figure (C) has largest number of sides, i.e. 8.

17. *(b)* If Cyra arranges the remaining toothpicks in the given manner, then she will get six triangles.

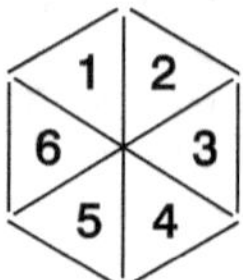

So, Cyra needs to use 2 slanting toothpicks and 1 standing toothpick.

18. *(b)* Number of cones △ $= 12$

Number of cylinders ▯ $= 6$

∴ Required difference $= 12 - 6 = 6$

19. *(c)* 1. All sides of a square are <u>equal</u>.
   2. A cuboid has <u>12</u> edges.
   3. There are <u>0</u> corners in a cylinder.
   4. A pole is an example of a <u>cylinder</u>.

20. *(d)*
   1. True.
   2. False, the given figure has 2 cubes and 1 cuboid.
   3. True.
   4. False, a cone has 1 corner and a sphere have 0 corner.

9. Pattern

1. *(b)* Let △ = A; ▢ = B; ◯ = C

Then, given question pattern is as follows

A B C   A B C   ⟦A B C⟧

So, C = ◯ will be the next term in the given question pattern.

Hence, option (b) is correct.

2. *(b)* Let, = A; = B;

Then, given question pattern is as follows

A B C   A B C   A ⟦B⟧ C

So, B = △ will be the next term in the given question pattern.

Hence, option (b) is correct.

3. *(a)* Let

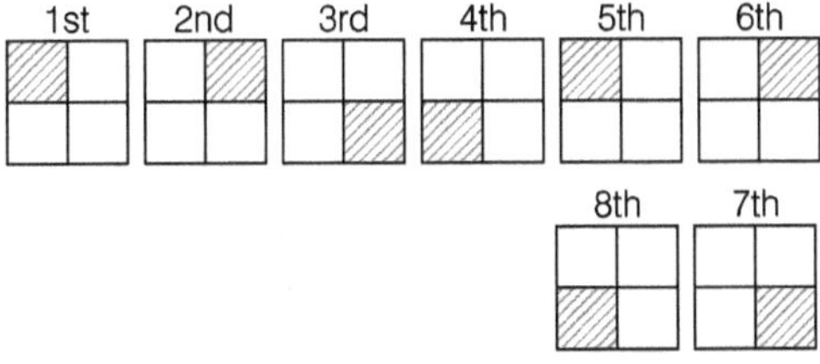

A = ⊘ ; B = ⊖ ; C = ⊗

Then, the given question pattern is as follows

  A B C   A B⊡   A ⊡ C
               (i)   (ii)

∴ (i) C = ⊗   Hence, option (a) is
                correct.

(ii) B = ⊖

4. *(a)* Here, the pattern is repeating itself after 3 steps. So, Mona's next step will be same as 2nd step. Hence, option a is correct.

5. *(a)* Here, the beads at odd number of places are black and the beads at even number of places are white.

Thus, the bead at 21st place is black, because 21 is an odd number,

6. *(b)* The terms in the option (a), (c) and (d) follow the similar pattern as AABAABAAB. But in option (b) the pattern is AAABAAABAAAB.

So, option (b) is different.

7. *(a)* The pattern in the given question is as follows

  1st   2nd   3rd   4th   5th   6th

                                8th   7th

Hence, option (a) is correct.

8. *(b)* The key has the following code

○ △ □ △ ○ □

Given, ○ = A, △ = B and □ = C

So, the pattern on key is ABC BAC.

Then, the lock which can be opened by the given key is the lock with the

letters ABC BAC which is in option (b).

Hence, option (b) is correct.

9. *(d)* The number of triangles is increasing in each figure.

   Ist figure = 1; IInd figure = 2
IIIrd figure = 3; IVth figure = 4
Similarly, Vth figure = 5
So, in Vth figure, there are 5 triangles.
Hence, option(d) is correct.

10. *(b)* The number of arrows is increasing in each figure.

Figure 1st → 2; Figure 2nd → 3
Figure 3rd → 4; Figure 4th → 5
Figure 5th → 6
So, in 5th figure there are 6 arrows.
Hence, option (b) is correct.

11. *(c)* First, third and fifth figure have same number of dots.

In second , fourth and sixth figure dots is increasing by 1.

So, 6th figure is wrong.

 → This should be the 6th figure.

Hence, option (c) is incorrect.

12. *(d)* In the given pattern, the number of sides in each shape is increasing by one and the face expression also changes. So, the pattern followed by the shapes is number of sides.

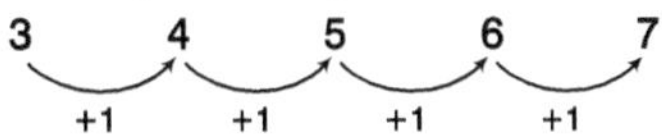

   3   4   5   6   7
    +1   +1   +1   +1

So, the next term will be

13. *(a)* Here, the arrow head is rotating from one line to the next in clockwise direction in which clock rotate.

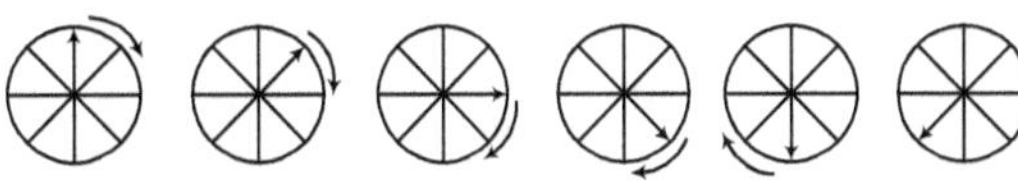

Hence, option (a) is correct.

14. *(a)* Here, the missing part of the figure is as follows 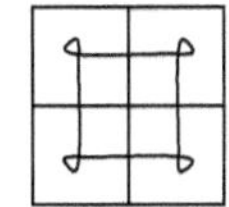

15. *(c)* Number of partition is decreasing in the pattern.

So, option (c) will be the correct answer.

16. *(c)* Here, in the given pattern the number of circles is decreasing by 1 end position of triangle is fix.

So, the next term in the given pattern is

5   4   3   2
   −1   −1   −1

i.e., 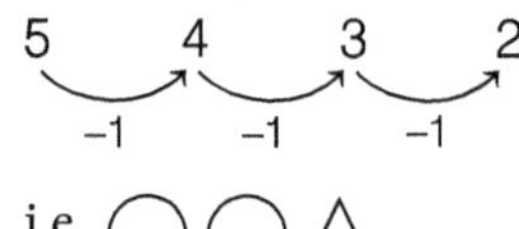

Hence, option (c) is correct.

17. *(b)* The numbers marked on the number lines are 0, 5, 10, 15.

Then, the pattern is as follows:

$$0 + 5 = 5;\ 5 + 5 = 10;\ 10 + 5 = 15$$

So, the number line shows skip counting by 5.

Hence, option (b) is correct.

18. *(c)* The given pattern shows skip counting by 10.

i.e.,
$$339 + 10 = 349$$
$$349 + 10 = \boxed{359}$$
$$359 + 10 = 369$$
$$369 + 10 = \boxed{379}$$

So, the missing number are 359, 379.

Hence, option (c) is correct.

19. (b) In the given pattern, numbers and their opposite images are written and the number are increasing by 1, so the next term will be 6 and its opposite image ∂ written together.

i.e.,

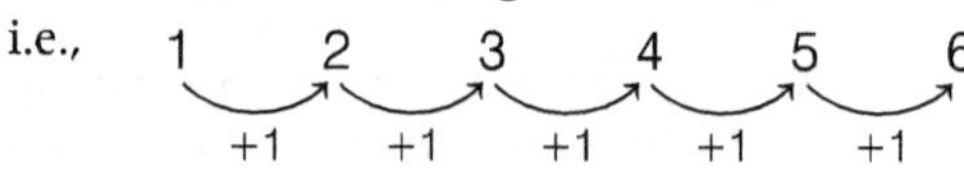

1   2   3   4   5   6
   +1   +1   +1   +1   +1

So, we get   6∂

Hence, option (b) is correct.

20. *(b)* The pattern is as follows:

In 1st figure, $2 \times 8 = 16$

and in 2nd figure, $4 \times A = 28$

∴ $A = 7$ [∵ $4 \times 7 = 28$]

21. *(d)* In 3rd figure, $3 \times 9 = 27$

$$B = 27$$

So, $A + B = 7 + 27 = 34$

10. Data Handling

1. *(d)* The given figures drawn by Lisa consists of 5 circles, 5 triangles, 3 squares and 2 rectangles.

∴ $A = 5,$ $B = 5,$ $C = 2,$ $D = 3$

2. *(d)* Number of ladybirds collected by Crispin = 6

Number of ladybirds collected by Clio = 7

Number of ladybirds collected by Kato = 7

Number of ladybirds collected by Lewis = 11

From the above data, it is clear that Lewis wins the game.

3. *(a)* We know that, Crispin collected the least number of ladybirds i.e., 6. [from the above data]

So, Crispin loses the game.

4. *(b)* Number of children who like chess = 3

Number of children who like drafts = 4

Number of children who like risk = 2

∴ Total number of children who like chess, drafts and risk = 3 + 4 + 2 = 9

It is given that 15 children voted for their favourite board game.

∴ Number of children who like monopoly
$$= 15 - 9 = 6$$

5. *(d)* Number of cakes sold on Monday
$$= 1\bigcirc$$
$$= 1 \times 2 = 2$$

Number of cakes sold on Tuesday
$$= 3\bigcirc = 3 \times 2 = 6$$

Number of cakes sold on Wednesday
$$= 5\bigcirc = 5 \times 2 = 10$$

Number of cakes sold on Thursday
$$= 4\bigcirc = 4 \times 2 = 8$$

Number of cakes sold on Friday
$$= 6\bigcirc = 6 \times 2 = 12$$

∴ Total number of cakes sold in this week
$$= 2 + 6 + 10 + 8 + 12 = 38$$

Solutions (Q. Nos. 6 and 7)

Number of shoppers who travelled by
$$\text{Car} = 5 \;\text{\Large\textsf{?}} = 5 \times 2 = 10$$
Number of shoppers who travelled by
$$\text{Bus} = 6 \;\text{\Large\textsf{?}} = 6 \times 2 = 12$$
Number of shoppers who travelled by
$$\text{Walk} = 2 \;\text{\Large\textsf{?}} = 2 \times 2 = 4$$
Number of shoppers who travelled by
$$\text{Bicycle} = 4 \;\text{\Large\textsf{?}} = 4 \times 2 = 8$$

6. *(b)* From the above information, we have
People travelled by bus $= 12$
People travelled by car $= 10$

∴ Required difference $= 12 - 10 = 2$

7. *(d)* We have,
Total number of shoppers who travelled by car, bus, walk and bicycle
$$= 10 + 12 + 4 + 8 = 34$$
and number of shoppers Bhevya surveyed $= 40$
∴ Number of shoppers who used other than the given transport $= 40 - 34 = 6$

8. *(c)* Number of Goat $= 4 \times 2 = 8$
Number of Cow $= 3 \times 3 = 9$
Number of Chicken $= 5 \times 1 = 5$
Number of Horse $= 1 \times 4 = 4$
Number of pig $= 2 \times 3 = 6$
So, Horse is fewest among all.

9. *(a)* From the above calculation,
Total number of animals in Daniel's farm
$$= 8 + 9 + 5 + 4 + 6 = 32$$

10. *(c)* Number of trees planted by Theon $= 5$
Number of trees planted by Cody $= 5$
Number of trees planted by John $= 4$
Number of trees planted by Jonas $= 5$
Number of trees planted by Cyrus $= 7$
∴ Total number of trees planted by all the students $= 5 + 5 + 4 + 5 + 7 = 26$
It is given that the students need to plant 30 trees in all.
∴ Number of more trees to be planted
$$= 30 - 26 = 4$$

11. *(d)* From the given data, it is clear that Cyrus planted maximum trees i.e. 7, Theon and Jonas planted the same number of trees i.e. 5 and John planted the least number of trees i.e. 4.
So, option (d) is correct.

12. *(d)* We have,
Number of cards Philo has $= 6$
$$= 6 \times 50 = 300$$
Number of cards Cosmo has $= 5$
$$= 5 \times 50 = 250$$
Number of cards Marcus has $= 7$
$$= 7 \times 50 = 350$$
Number of cards Nero has $= 4$
$$= 4 \times 50 = 200$$
So, Philo $\rightarrow$ C; Cosmo $\rightarrow$ A;
Marcus $\rightarrow$ D; Nero $\rightarrow$ B

13. *(d)* Arranging the electricity bills in ascending order, we get
$$324 < 356 < 365 < 400 < 435 < 548 < 617$$
$$< 700 < 736 < 780$$
So, 780 is the highest amount.
Hence, the electricity bill of 780 is of the 10th house.

14. *(b)* From the given table, it is clear that Peri is the tallest girl as her height is 112 centimetres.
and Suzanne is second tallest, since her height is 108 centimetres.
Also, from the given queue, we have

So, Suzanne is on the 2nd position in the queue.

15. *(b)* We have,
Increases in height of tree from March to April
$$= 50 - 20 = 30 \text{ centimetres}$$

Increases in height of tree from April to May
$$= 100 - 50 = 50 \text{ centimetres}$$
Increases in height of tree from May to June
$$= 120 - 100 = 20 \text{ centimetres}$$
Increases in height of tree from June to July
$$= 160 - 120 = 40 \text{ centimetres}$$
Thus, in the month of May, height of the tree increase the most.

16. *(b)* From the above calculation, it is clear that the overall increases in the height of tree from March till July
$$= 30 + 50 + 20 + 40$$
$$= 140 \text{ centimetres}$$

17. *(d)* Number of students engaged in cycling
$$= 36$$
Number of students engaged in running $= 19$
Number of students engaged in swimming
$$= 23$$
Number of students engaged in music $= 6$
So, Clearly we can see that
maximum number of students engaged in cycling

minimum number of students engaged in music.
option (d) is correct.

18. *(b)* Number of students engaged in cycling
$$= 36$$
$\therefore$ Number of students engaged in swimming
$$= 23$$
$\because$ Number of students engaged in both activities together = Students in cycling
$$+ \text{ Students in swimming}$$
$$= 36 + 23 = 59$$

19. *(a)* Sunset time on 4th July $= 6 : 00$ pm
Sunrise time on 4th July $= 5 : 30$ am
$\therefore$ Required time difference
$$= 6 : 00 \text{ pm} - 5 : 30 \text{ am} = 12 \text{ hours } 30 \text{ min}$$

20. *(c)* Sunset time on 2nd July $= 7 : 00$ pm
Sunset time on 4th July $= 6 : 00$ pm
$\therefore$ Time difference $= 7 : 00 \text{ pm} - 6 : 00 \text{ pm}$
$$= 1 \text{ hour} = 60 \text{ minutes}$$
So, sunset 60 minutes earlier on 4th July then on 2nd July.

Answers

Practice Set 1

1. (a)	2. (d)	3. (c)	4. (c)	5. (c)	6. (a)	7. (d)	8. (d)	9. (a)	10. (b)
11. (b)	12. (b)	13. (a)	14. (c)	15. (d)	16. (c)	17. (a)	18. (c)	19. (a)	20. (b)
21. (b)	22. (d)	23. (b)	24. (b)	25. (a)	26. (c)	27 (d)	28. (d)	29 (b)	30 (a)
31. (b)	32. (b)	33. (b)	34. (c)	35. (b)					

Practice Set 2

1. (a)	2. (c)	3. (c)	4. (c)	5. (b)	6. (b)	7. (c)	8. (d)	9. (d)	10. (a)
11. (a)	12. (d)	13. (c)	14. (b)	15. (b)	16. (d)	17. (a)	18. (c)	19. (c)	20. (d)
21. (b)	22. (d)	23. (a)	24. (b)	25. (d)	26. (a)	27 (c)	28. (b)	29 (c)	30 (d)
31. (a)	32. (a)	33. (b)	34. (c)	35. (a)					